The Insanity Defense: A Blueprint For Legislative Reform

The Insanity Defense: A Blueprint For Legislative Reform

Grant H. Morris
University of San Diego

Lexington Books
D.C. Heath and Company
Lexington, Massachusetts
Toronto London

Library of Congress Cataloging in Publication Data

Morris, Grant H. 1940-
The insanity defense.

Includes bibliographical references and index.
1. Insanity—Jurisprudence—United States. 2. Insanity—Jurisprudence—New York (State) 3. Forensic psychiatry. I. Title.
KF9242.M6 345'.73'04 75-14869
ISBN 0-669-00054-x

Published simultaneously in Canada

Printed in the United States of America

International Standard Book Number: 0-669-00054-x

Library of Congress Catalog Card Number: 75-14869

To the memory of my father, Benjamin Morris—an attorney who believed in and practiced moral responsibility.

Contents

Preface

My first practical exposure to the insanity defense did not involve its courtroom presentation by a defendant attempting to avoid responsibility for criminal conduct. Rather the experience concerned the fate of Oscar Z., who had been acquitted through use of this defense and who, as a result, was confined in Matteawan State Hospital. That institution is a maximum security mental hospital housing various categories of so-called criminal-order mental patients. The post-acquittal process to which Oscar Z. was subjected created an unjust situation that was remedied through a minor change in existing legislation.

On February 15, 1965, Oscar Z. wrote a letter to the New York Department of Mental Hygiene, requesting consideration for transfer from Matteawan to a civil state hospital.[1] Matteawan is under the jurisdiction of the New York Department of Correction; the civil state hospitals are under the jurisdiction of the New York Department of Mental Hygiene. Because correction facilities emphasize security, even at the expense of treatment, transfer to a civil hospital would significantly increase Oscar Z.'s opportunities for psychiatric therapy.

At the time Oscar Z. wrote his letter, I was employed by the Institute of Public Administration, working in the Office of Counsel of the Department of Mental Hygiene on a special project to revise and recodify the New York Mental Hygiene Law. Although the laws involving criminal-order patients were tangential to our project, we were intrigued by Oscar Z.'s plight. He had been indicted for grand larceny, first degree, on October 29, 1947, but at trial was found not guilty by reason of insanity. On December 1, 1949, the court ordered him committed to Matteawan State Hospital "until he shall become sane." The court acted pursuant to Code of Criminal Procedure section 454, which mandated Matteawan confinement for persons acquitted by reason of insanity.

On March 1, 1954, Oscar Z. was examined by a psychiatrist, Robert C. Hunt, M.D., an Assistant Commissioner of the Department of Mental Hygiene. The examination report disclosed that the patient had no history of violence. His present mental condition was described as "quiet, preoccupied, disinterested, laughs and talks to himself, admits auditory hallucinations." Nevertheless the psychiatrist concluded: "Since the patient is in Matteawan on Section 454 of the Code of Criminal Procedure there is no legal provision under which he can be transferred to a civil State hospital."

In 1960, section 454 was amended[2] to include, among other things, a provision authorizing the transfer to civil state hospitals of insanity-acquitted patients confined in Matteawan.[3]

A document dated February 19, 1963, signed by L. Groth, M.D., states that Oscar Z. "showed a willingness and cooperativeness to work as a tailor. He has not acted out any violent trends during the past year." An unsigned document written the following year notes that Oscar Z. "is not a management problem. He is described as a steady and good ward worker, neat and clean, seclusive, watches television and spends a great deal of time reading." Clearly, Oscar Z. was not a security problem and therefore was an appropriate candidate for transfer to a civil state hospital. Nevertheless, his 1965 request for transfer was rejected. L. Laramour Bryan, M.D., Assistant Commissioner of the Department of Mental Hygiene, wrote this notation on Oscar Z.'s letter: "This patient was admitted to Matteawan State Hospital 9-17-49 and apparently is not eligible for transfer to a Civil State Hospital assuming that amended § 454 is not retroactive??"

I was informed by E. David Wiley, Legal Counsel of the Department of Mental Hygiene, that amended section 454 would be applied only prospectively—that is, only to those insanity-acquitted patients placed in Matteawan after the effective date of the legislative change. Thus, five patients, including Oscar Z., who were placed in Matteawan prior to September 1, 1960, and who were still there in 1965, were not eligible for transfer. Mr. Wiley explained that the amended statute contained new provisions authorizing the court to place conditions on the discharge of an insanity-acquitted patient[4] and empowering the court to revoke that conditional release within five years.[5] Retroactive application of those restrictive provisions might subject the statute to attack as an unconstitutional ex post facto law.[6]

Even if the Department's position on the restrictive provisions of the 1960 legislation was tenable, other provisions of the legislation, including the one authorizing transfer of insanity-acquitted patients from Matteawan to the civil state hospitals, could have applied retrospectively. However the Department refused to so construe the legislation.

When the staff of the recodification project learned of Oscar Z.'s situation, we considered various measures to make him eligible for transfer as quickly as possible. Our decision was to pursue legislative change rather than to litigate the issue of retroactivity in the courts. The vehicle of our attempt was section 409 of the New York Correction Law. The statute dealt with Matteawan-confined, insane prisoners upon expiration of their term of imprisonment. They were to be retained in Matteawan until they recovered.[7] Section 409 was most conducive to our purpose because at the time bills were pending in the New York State Legislature that would make minor changes in the statute.[8]

The recodification staff amended these bills after obtaining the consent and support of Assemblyperson Kenneth L. Wilson and Senator R. Watson Pomeroy, who had first introduced the bills; the Department of Correction, which had sponsored the original bill; the Department of Mental Hygiene, which would receive patients pursuant to our amendment; and W. Cecil Johnston, M.D., Superintendent of Matteawan. Our amendment empowered the Commissioner of Correction, with the consent of the Commissioner of Mental Hygiene, to transfer from Matteawan to a civil state hospital any unrecovered, mentally ill non-prisoner patient not charged with a crime.[9] Under this amendment, Oscar Z. and other insanity-acquitted patients confined in Matteawan prior to September 1960 would be eligible for transfer. We also added this language:

> All provisions of the mental hygiene law governing patients civilly admitted to institutions in the department of mental hygiene, including trial release, convalescent status and discharge, shall apply to all patients transferred to institutions in the department of mental hygiene pursuant to this section.[10]

The bills passed both houses of the New York State Legislature and were transmitted to Governor Nelson A. Rockefeller for his signature. His office then raised a technical objection to the wording of the bills that required their recall less than twenty-four hours before they would have become law without the governor's signature. The vote in the Assembly was reconsidered, and the Assembly bill was amended to meet the objection.[11] The Assembly passed the amended bill on the day before the legislative session was to adjourn. The Senate passed it on the final day of the session. Nearly a month later, the governor signed the bill into law.[12] Seven months after the bill became law, Oscar Z. was transferred to Manhattan State Hospital, which is a civil hospital.

A letter dated May 27, 1966, sent from Dr. Bryan to the Honorable Paul D. McGinnis, Commissioner of Correction, offers an ironic postscript to the Oscar Z. story:

> In 1965, §409 of the Correction Law was amended to permit transfer of non-prisoner patients from Matteawan to civil state hospitals, upon the order of the Commissioner of Correction with the consent of the Commissioner of Mental Hygiene. The transfer of Oscar Z. should have been effected through operation of §409 of the Correction Law, and not through the amended provision of §454 of the Code of Criminal Procedure.
>
> Therefore, I would appreciate it if you would regularize the transfer of Oscar Z. from Matteawan State Hospital to Manhattan State Hospital by issuing the proper order of transfer and dating it, January 21, 1966.

Although the Department of Mental Hygiene had decided that the transfer provision of amended Code of Criminal Procedure section 454 could not be applied retroactively to include Oscar Z. and although Correction Law section 409 was amended to specifically authorize transfer pursuant to its terms, Oscar Z. was apparently transferred pursuant to section 454.

The postscript to the Oscar Z. story could lead the reader to conclude that efforts to secure legislative reform are inconsequential. However, I do not want to create that impression. Despite the irregularities in the paperwork surrounding Oscar Z.'s transfer, he did become eligible for transfer through the legislative change itself. Obtaining this change and completing the transfer were accomplished in far less time than would have elapsed if the Department of Mental Hygiene's restrictive interpretation of section 454 had been litigated in the courts.

A significant insight I gained from my experience with Oscar Z. is that at least in his case the legislative process was conciliatory; people with divergent views collaborated in order to solve a problem. The legislative process established a mood that promoted objective, unemotional decision making by administrators in implementing the legislative policy. In contrast, the litigation process is adversarial; an opponent is attacked because of the position he takes on an issue. The antagonism usually engendered by litigation is likely to continue after the court has declared one side to be the winner of the dispute. In the Oscar Z. example, our legislative change authorized, but did not require, the transfer of the patient. Nevertheless, the administrators in the Department of Mental Hygiene and Department of Correction responded affirmatively to the legislative grant of power by ordering the transfer of Oscar Z. The litigation we considered, if successful, would have also authorized, but not required, the transfer of the patient. However, I doubt that a court decision would have received the same positive response.

An epilogue to this experience with the insanity defense illustrates that legislative revision is a continuing process. In 1974, both the problem statute (section 454) and the solution statute (section 409) were amended, thereby ending all Matteawan confinement for insanity-acquittees and exconvict mental patients.[13] These people are now civil patients and as such can be confined only in civil state hospitals. This new legislation, prompted by an appellate court decision,[14] eliminates completely the Oscar Z. problem.

I do not offer legislation as a panacea. In the complex interface of criminal law and psychiatry, progress on problems of insanity defendants, who are doubly stigmatized as mentally ill and criminal, is rarely achieved through sweeping legislative reform. Nevertheless, legislation is a viable alternative to litigation and should be neither neglected nor disdained.

In 1974, the Criminal Code Commission of the Arizona State Legislature contacted me and requested that I prepare a report on the insanity defense. The report was to identify and analyze current academic, judicial, and legislative thought on the defense and to recommend reforms of the law. My experience with Oscar Z. suggested that such a study would be a worthwhile endeavor, and I therefore accepted the invitation. That report forms the basis of this book.

My emphasis here is on the practical, not the theoretical. I attempt to educate the reader on the various insanity defense themes and then to suggest workable reforms appropriate for our society. My book's success can be measured only by its ability to influence legislatures to pass enlightened legislation. It is to that task I now turn.

Notes

1. Portions of the Oscar Z. story were published originally as Appendix C of Morris, *The Confusion of Confinement Syndrome Extended: The Treatment of Mentally Ill "Non-Criminal Criminals" in New York*, 18 BUFF. L. REV. 393, 436-39 (1969). © 1969 by the Buffalo Law Review. Reprinted with permission. Copies of all documents mentioned in the Oscar Z. story are on file with the author.

2. N.Y. Sess. Laws 1960, ch. 550, § 1, effective September 1, 1960.

3. *Id.*

4. *Id.* N.Y. Sess. Laws 1970, ch. 996, § 1 recodified and renumbered the statutes without substantive change. The conditional release provision in now N.Y. CRIM PROC. LAW § 330.20(3) (McKinney 1971).

5. N.Y. Sess. Laws 1960, ch. 550, § 1. The provision authorizing revocation of conditional release was renumbered by N.Y. Sess. Laws 1970, ch. 996, § 1 and is now N.Y. CRIM. PRO. LAW § 330.20(4) (McKinney 1971).

6. U.S. CONST. art. I, § 9 prohibits Congress from passing an ex post facto law, and U.S. CONST. art. I, § 10 imposes the same prohibition on the states.

7. N.Y. Sess. Laws 1929, ch. 243, § 18.

8. N.Y. Ass. Intro. No. 2656, Ass. Print No. 2662 (Feb. 17, 1965); N.Y. Sen. Intro. No. 1363, Sen. Print No. 1377 (Feb. 17, 1965).

9. N.Y. Ass. Intro. No. 2656, Ass. Print No. 6318 (Apr. 7, 1965); N.Y. Sen. Intro. No. 1363, Sen. Print No. 4937 (Apr. 7, 1965).

10. N.Y. Ass. Intro. No. 2656, Ass. Print No. 6318 (Apr. 7, 1965); N.Y. Sen. Intro. No. 1363, Sen. Print No. 4937 (Apr. 7, 1965).

11. N.Y. Ass. Intro. No. 2656, Ass. Print No. 7315 (June 15, 1965).

12. N.Y. Sess. Laws 1965, ch. 879.

13. N.Y. Sess. Laws 1974, ch. 629, §§ 3 and 4.

14. Kesselbrenner v. Anonymous, 33 N.Y.2d 161, 305 N.E.2d 903, 350 N.Y.S.2d 889 (1973).

Acknowledgments

I would like to thank: Professor David B. Wexler, University of Arizona College of Law, for recommending to the Criminal Code Commission of the Arizona State Legislature that I be appointed a consultant to prepare a report on the insanity defense; Mr. Warren K. Smoot, Director of that Commission, who appointed me and who assisted in overcoming difficulties in preparing the report and the book; the Executive Committee of the Arizona Legislative Council, who granted me permission to copyright the report; Mr. Alan Brubaker and Mr. Donald Christensen, law students who did valuable research for this project; Ms. Marilyn Riley, a perfect pedant, who edited the book and would not let a sentence rest until its wording met with her satisfaction; Ms. Rockie McKee, my secretary, who in her own "cheerful" way did an excellent job of typing the manuscript; and most of all, my family: my wife, Phyllis, who put up with my ranting and raving during this project and all previous ones, and my children, Joshua and Sara, who will love to see their names in print.

The Insanity Defense: A Blueprint For Legislative Reform

1 General Considerations

The Purposes and Functions of the Insanity Defense

Our criminal law is premised on this assumption: Because an individual has the ability to choose between socially acceptable and socially unacceptable behavior, he can be held responsible for conduct that violates the law. Thus, an individual who chooses to commit a crime is morally blameworthy, and he is therefore an appropriate subject for punishment.

The concept of free will embodied in the criminal law has been criticized by those who subscribe to the view that all behavior is "determined by psychological and biological causative factors."[1] A focal point of the moralist-determinist debate is the insanity defense, for implicit in the defense is society's admission that a serious mental condition may destroy a person's free will and that moral condemnation is not appropriate in such circumstances.

In any insanity defense discussion, the battle between moralists and determinists is a primary concern. However, the insanity defense itself must be placed into the broader context of generally accepted criminal law principles. Whatever the merits of the determinists' arguments, free will generally reigns supreme in the enactment of criminal laws, in the determination of guilt, and even in the sentencing process. As Mr. Justice Robert H. Jackson wrote:

> How far one by an exercise of free will may determine his general destiny or his course in a particular matter and how far he is the toy of circumstance has been debated through the ages by theologians, philosophers, and scientists. Whatever doubts they have entertained as to the matter, the practical business of government and administration of the law is obliged to proceed on more or less rough and ready judgments based on the assumption that mature and rational persons are in control of their own conduct.[2]

The insanity defense excludes from criminal responsibility those individuals whose mental condition is such that a finding of guilt would not serve the purposes of the criminal law. However, as one noted authority has stated: "Unfortunately, we are at a point in history when it is not at all clear what those purposes are and, therefore, what the function of the insanity defense is or should be."[3]

Although punishment is explained and justified by several theories, the insanity defense has been construed as consistent with each.[4] The *prevention theory* (specific deterrence) is premised on the assertion that subjecting the individual to the highly unpleasant experience of imprisonment or other sanction will deter him from engaging in future crimes because he will not want to be punished again. This theory assumes the individual is able to comprehend the sanctions imposed on law violators and to respond accordingly. A severely disordered person may not be so deterred. However, the existence of the insanity defense coupled with hospitalization of the individual who successfully raises the defense affords society the opportunity to treat him and thus reduce his potential for repetition of criminal conduct.

The *deterrence theory* (general prevention) attempts to reinforce the public's law-abiding tendencies by punishing those individuals who have not been law-abiding. Because non-criminal, non-insane individuals do not identify with the insane defendant, he does not serve as an appropriate deterrence example for the public.

Under the *rehabilitation theory*, sanctions are imposed to alter a person's behavior to a pattern that is socially acceptable. The insanity defense, coupled with hospitalization following acquittal, permits rehabilitation of the mentally disordered person through appropriate treatment techniques.

The *restraint theory* is based on the need to protect society from dangerous individuals. Hospitalization following acquittal by reason of insanity fulfills this purpose because the individual is detained, not for some fixed period of time but indefinitely, until he is no longer dangerous.

The *retribution theory*, which has recently been criticized, asserts the appropriateness of society's inflicting suffering on one who has inflicted suffering on others. Criminal culpability generally requires *mens rea*—that is, an intent to commit a criminal act. Severely mentally disordered individuals are considered not blameworthy because they lack the capacity (free will) to form this criminal intent. The insanity defense developed as a device to preclude retributive punishment of these individuals whom society views as not blameworthy.

Proposals to Abolish the Insanity Defense

It is one thing to say that the insanity defense coupled with hospitalization after acquittal is consistent with the purposes of the criminal law: It is quite another to decide on the purpose of the defense itself. A general assumption underlying the insanity defense is that it enables society to distinguish ". . . between the cases where a punitive-correctional disposition is appropriate and those in which a medical-custodial disposition is the only kind that the law should allow."[5] A dividing line is drawn between the criminal offender and the insanity-acquittee. The former receives public condemnation through a criminal conviction with resulting punitive sanctions; the latter receives no public condemnation but is restrained for treatment of his mental condition to insure the anti-social conduct is not repeated.

Some authorities believe that the insanity defense is not an appropriate device for drawing this line and that the defense should be abolished. The insanity defense allows introduction into the criminal trial of psychiatric testimony concerning the accused's mental condition at the time the criminal act was committed. These authorities contend this testimony is not relevant if the ultimate goal of the criminal trial is appropriate disposition of the individual. The insanity defense says nothing of the accused's current mental condition or of the probability that the condition is treatable in a mental hospital. Thus, these authorities argue that the criminal trial should be conducted without psychiatric input on the issue of legal accountability and that psychiatric insight should be reserved for a post-conviction analysis of proper disposition of the offender.[6]

Other abolitionists question whether a line should be drawn at all between confinement of convicts in prison and confinement of non-convict acquittees in mental hospitals. To these abolitionists, the appropriate choice is significantly different. If the commission of a crime requires both the commission of a criminal act and a criminal intent to commit that act, the individual who lacks criminal intent because his mental condition deprived him of free will is simply not guilty of a crime. The insanity defense, coupled as it is with commitment of the acquitted individual to a mental hospital, is viewed as a device inappropriately to confine individuals who should go free. Generally, unless all the elements of an offense can be proven against an individual, he can be neither convicted nor confined. Thus the insanity defense does not

> . . . absolve of criminal responsibility "sick" persons who would otherwise be subject to criminal sanction. Rather, its real function is to authorize the state to hold those "who must be found not to possess the guilty mind *mens rea*," even though the criminal law demands that no person be held criminally responsible if doubt is cast on any material element of the offense charged.[7]

These authorities would limit evidence of an accused's mental condition ". . . to the question of whether he did or did not, at the time of the act, have the prohibited *mens rea* of the crime of which he is charged."[8]

Both abolitionist positions have been subjected to attack. In his definitive book on the insanity defense, Dean Abraham S. Goldstein criticizes the first position discussed above. He cites four major objections to separating the offending act from the mental state of the offender and reserving evidence of mental condition for the dispositional portion of the trial.[9] First, the jurisdictions that have attempted this have been singularly unsuccessful. Courts have held that evidence concerning the *mens rea* element may not be excluded from the guilt-finding portion of the criminal trial.[10] Thus, evidence of the defendant's mental condition has been admitted in both portions of the trial, and in essence the defendant has been accorded the opportunity to prove his insanity twice.[11] Two state legislatures—Washington in 1909 and Mississippi in 1928—attempted to eliminate both the insanity defense and the requirement of *mens rea*. The statutes, struck down almost immediately by the states' supreme courts, were held to unconstitutionally deny due process of law by depriving defendants of a jury trial on defenses that had always been considered by the jury.[12] In 1928, Louisiana enacted a statute providing for a trial before a lunacy commission if the defendant pleaded insanity. If the commission found the defendant sane, he was precluded from raising the insanity defense at a subsequent trial before a jury. One year after its enactment, the Louisiana Supreme Court held the statute unconstitutional as violating both due process and the right to a jury trial.[13]

The second major objection is that a proposal to defer consideration of a defendant's mental condition to the dispositional stage would result in convicting some individuals who are now acquitted because they lack *mens rea*. Experience indicates ". . . that prematurely labeling a person an 'offender' is more likely than any other single factor to confirm him in a criminal career . . . ."[14] Unfortunately, our society has not yet accepted Chief Justice Joseph Weintraub's admonition that we should " . . . think of the adjudication of guilt as nothing more than a finding that this mortal has demonstrated his capacity to do harm, the need for segregating him or otherwise treating him or dealing with him. . . ."[15]

Third, keeping alive the concept of blame is essential to the continued order of society, for this concept fosters individual responsibility. In our culture, the principle of blameworthiness establishes the limits beyond which nonconformity may not go. Without such limits, society would become less law-abiding. By giving a person the opportunity to contest his blameworthiness through the device of the insanity defense, society reinforces the individual's sense of obligation. The individual is not viewed as a programmed machine who has been acted upon by forces beyond his control; rather he is assumed responsible for his own judgments unless the contrary is established. A proposal to reserve for dispositional use only evidence of a person's mental condition would erode the concept of blameworthiness and therefore weaken the moral order.

Fourth, for blameworthiness to remain the basis of continued social order, the decision to impose official condemnation through conviction or to show compassion through acquittal must be made by a jury rather than by a panel of experts. The public identifies with the jury and is influenced by jury decisions. Eliminating the insanity defense from the jury's consideration would deprive it of this symbolic function.

The second abolitionist position discussed above regards the insanity defense as a device to confine innocent individuals who should have been found not guilty of a crime because they lacked criminal intent required for its commission. This position has been attacked as being overly inclusive. At times the circumstances establishing a successful insanity defense may also establish that the defendant did not have the mental state required for conviction of a crime; however, this is not always the case. For example, certain strict liability crimes require no proof of a criminal intent in order to convict the defendant. If such a crime was charged, a defendant could not avoid criminal liability by asserting lack of *mens rea*, but he could do so by successfully establishing an insanity defense. The concept of *mens rea* centers on a particular mental state (such as intent, knowledge, recklessness, or negligence) that is a necessary element of most crimes. The insanity defense is a broader concept, requiring an examination of the accused's general mental condition.[16]

The strengths and weaknesses of the position of those who would eliminate the insanity defense and focus solely on *mens rea* are clearly demonstrated by the following example from Professors Wayne R. LaFave and Austin W. Scott, Jr.:

> Thus, at one extreme, if the effect of the defendant's mental disease was that he did not even know what he was doing—if, to take an oft-cited example, he strangled his wife but believed that he was squeezing lemons—he would certainly have a valid insanity defense under any of the insanity tests now in use. But, in a homicide prosecution which included as an element of the charge that the defendant killed his wife intentionally, knowingly, or recklessly (defined in subjective terms, in that the defendant was actually aware of the risk attending his actions), it would also be correct to say that this defendant is simply not guilty for lack of *mens rea*. At least to the extent that courts have declined to admit evidence of mental disease except in the context of an insanity defense, it could be said that in this situation the defense serves as a device for committing those who would otherwise be acquitted.
>
> At the other extreme, if the effect of the defendant's mental disease was that he was significantly lacking in the ability to control his actions, he would again have an insanity defense under at least some of the insanity tests. But it is unlikely that it could be said that this defendant, merely because of limitations upon his powers of self-control, did not act with intent (that is, with a purpose of bringing about the harmful result), knowledge (awareness that the harmful result would follow), or recklessness (awareness of a substantial risk that the harmful risk will follow), whatever the relevant mental state is for the offense charged. In such a situation, the insanity defense serves as a means to bring about commitment of the defendant in lieu of conviction and imprisonment.[17]

In subsequent portions of this book,[18] I will discuss more extensively arguments for greater utilization of evidence relating to defendant's mental state even though his mental condition does not meet the requirements of the jurisdiction's insanity test.

Significance of the Insanity Defense

The mental condition of a person accused of a crime may be raised in two different determinations. The first determination is defendant's competency to stand trial. Here the court examines the accused's *present* mental capacity to participate in the preparation and presentation of his defense to the criminal charge. The second determination is defendant's responsibility at the time the criminal act was committed. Here, through the insanity defense, the court or jury examines the accused's *past* mental capacity in order to determine whether criminal condemnation is appropriate. Of the two issues, the latter has received the most attention from scholars. However, the significance of the insanity defense has recently been questioned. As Professor Norval Morris eloquently stated:

> Rivers of ink, mountains of printer's lead, forests of paper have been expended on this issue [the insanity defense], which is surely marginal to the chaotic problem of effective, rational, and humane prevention and treatment of crime.[19]

There are at least two reasons for asserting that the importance of the insanity defense has been exaggerated. First, the inquiry into competency to stand trial has traditionally been the critical phase in classifying and disposing of cases involving mentally disturbed defendants.[20] Studies in various states disclose that criminal defendants have been found incompetent to stand trial and confined in maximum security mental facilities as an expedient final disposition of the charges against them.[21] A Michigan study reveals that well over one-half of the people committed to a maximum security facility as incompetent to stand trial could expect to spend the rest of their lives confined there with no change in status. This finding is not unique.[22]

A second reason for asserting that the insanity defense is relatively unimportant concerns the practical choice facing a defendant:

> The consequence of successful assertion of the defense in most jurisdictions is confinement in a maximum-security hospital with little prospect of care or early discharge. A defendant . . . would reasonably subject himself to such a disposition only if the alternative were capital punishment. . . .[A]ssertion of the defense appears to be directly associated with the severity of the offense and the therapeutic reputation of the maximum-security hospital in any particular jurisdiction.[23]

Nevertheless, recent developments suggest an increased importance of the defense. Three years ago, in *Jackson v. Indiana*,[24] the Supreme Court of the United States held

> . . . that a person charged by a State with a criminal offense who is committed solely on account of his incapacity to proceed to trial cannot be held more than the reasonable period of time necessary to determine whether there is a substantial probability that he will attain that capacity in the foreseeable future. If it is determined that this is not the case, then the State must either institute the customary civil commitment proceeding that would be required to commit indefinitely any other citizen, or release the defendant. Furthermore, even if it is determined that the defendant probably soon will be able to stand trial, his continued commitment must be justified by progress toward that goal.[25]

Because mentally disordered defendants can no longer be indeterminately and even permanently committed to a mental hospital as incompetent to stand trial, there are potentially more defendants who will be returned to court for trial and who will assert the insanity defense to avoid a finding of criminal responsibility.

Recently appellate courts in a number of jurisdictions[26] have ruled that commitment of insanity acquittees *for an indefinite period of time* is constitutionally impermissible unless they are afforded all the procedural safeguards available to those who are civilly committed. One court has specifically extended this requirement of equal procedural safeguards to the question of release by ruling that release from confinement may not be made more difficult for those acquitted by reason of insanity than for those civilly committed.[27]

If confinement for an indefinite period of time does not automatically follow an acquittal by reason of insanity, defendants who were mentally disordered at the time the criminal act was committed may be more willing to assert the insanity defense. These court decisions are discussed in a subsequent portion of this book.[28] Included in the discussion is the argument that if an individual is civilly committed after acquittal by reason of insanity, the conditions placed on his confinement should not be more restrictive than are conditions placed on other civilly committed patients. Obviously, if mentally disordered defendants do not face automatic confinement in a maximum security ward of a mental institution upon successfully pleading the insanity defense, they will be less reluctant to assert the defense.

Recommendations

In deciding if we should continue to utilize an insanity defense, we must consider whether there are any individuals who should be absolved from criminal responsibility because they are unable to conform to the demands of society. I believe that such individuals exist and that given society's current stage of development, the insanity defense is an appropriate device for dealing with them.

However, some abolitionists argue that having an insanity defense is senseless, for a mentally disordered individual who is absolved from criminal responsibility is then penalized by placement in a maximum security ward of a so-called mental hospital without treatment for an indefinite sentence that could continue for life. Their solution is to abolish the insanity defense and substitute the concept of *mens rea*. Such a solution would result in pure acquittal and release back into society of those individuals who have committed in the past—and who may continue to commit in the future—criminal acts without the requisite criminal intent. I reject this solution as potentially dangerous and therefore understandably unacceptable to society.

The strength of the abolitionists' argument lies not in their call for abolition of the insanity defense but rather in their assertion that society fails to make a meaningful distinction between the stigma of involuntary institutionalization due to conviction and the stigma of involuntary institutionalization due to mental abnormality. If the insanity defense is to be retained, this problem must be confronted.

I propose first that the insanity defense be retained and expanded to include those individuals whom an enlightened society would define as not criminally responsible. Second, whenever a crime requires as a necessary element that the act be committed with a particular mental state, evidence of a defendant's mental abnormality should be admissible to prove he lacked the required mental state, separate and apart from the insanity defense. This issue, often called *diminished responsibility*, will be discussed in greater detail in a subsequent portion of this book.[29] Third, legislative activity must be aimed not solely at revising the technical language utilized in the various formulations of the insanity test, but also at insuring fairness in the procedures for raising and determining the defense and reform in the system of disposing of those who successfully assert the defense.

If the purpose of the insanity defense is to find those individuals who are not criminally blameworthy, they should not subsequently be viewed as criminally blameworthy, sentence-serving convicts. Whether imposed by law or by practice, a requirement that an individual successfully pleading the insanity defense be committed to a maximum security facility for an indefinite time destroys any justification for the defense and reduces its significance to less than *de minimus*.

Notes

1. F. Alexander and H. Staub, THE CRIMINAL, THE JUDGE, AND THE PUBLIC 70-71 (New York: The MacMillan Co., 1931).

2. Gregg Cartage and Storage Co. v. United States, 316 U.S. 74, 79-80 (1941).

3. A. Goldstein, THE INSANITY DEFENSE 11 (New Haven: Yale University Press,1967). Reprinted with permission of Yale University Press. Copyright © by Yale University.

4. *Id.* at 12-15. *See generally* W. LaFave and A. Scott, HANDBOOK ON CRIMINAL LAW 271-72 (St. Paul: West Publishing Co., 1972).

5. MODEL PENAL CODE § 4.01, Comments, at 156 (Tent. Draft No. 4, 1955) (footnote omitted).

6. *See, e.g.*, H.L.A. Hart, THE MORALITY OF THE CRIMINAL LAW, ch. 1 (New York: Oxford University Press, 1965); K. Menninger, THE CRIME OF PUNISHMENT (New York: Viking Press, 1968); and B. Wooten, CRIME AND THE CRIMINAL LAW, ch. 2, 3 (London: Stevens and Sons, Ltd., 1963).

7. Goldstein and Katz, *Abolish the "Insanity Defense"—Why Not?*, 72 YALE L.J. 853, 864 (1963) (footnotes omitted).

8. Morris, *Psychiatry and the Dangerous Criminal*, 41 S. CAL. L. REV. 514, 518 (1968). The appendix to this article, *id.* at 544-47, lists the arguments of the various proponents of abolition.

9. A. Goldstein, *supra* note 3, at 222-26.

10. *See, e.g.*, People v. Wells, 33 Cal. 2d 330, 202 P.2d 53, *cert. denied*, 338 U.S. 836 (1949).

11. *See generally* Louisell and Hazard, *Insanity as a Defense: The Bifurcated Trial*, 49 CALIF. L. REV. 805 (1961).

12. State v. Strasberg, 60 Wash. 106, 110 P. 1020 (1910); Sinclair v. State, 161 Miss. 142, 132 So. 581 (1931).

13. State v. Lange, 168 La. 958, 123 So. 639 (1929).

14. A. Goldstein, *supra* note 3, at 223.

15. Weintraub, Remarks at Panel Discussion on Insanity as a Defense, Annual Judicial Conference of the Second Judicial Circuit, 37 F.R.D. 365, 371 (1964).

16. Brady, *Abolish the Insanity Defense?—No!*, 8 HOUSTON L. REV. 629, 642-43 (1971).

17. W. LaFave and A. Scott, *supra* note 4, at 270-71 (footnotes omitted).

18. *See* discussion in text pp. 7-8 and 75-83 *infra*.

19. Morris, *supra* note 8, at 516.

20. A. Matthews, MENTAL DISABILITY AND THE CRIMINAL LAW 193 (Chicago: American Bar Foundation, 1970).

21. *See, e.g.*, Morris, *The Confusion of Confinement Syndrome Extended: The Treatment of Mentally Ill "Non-Criminal Criminals" in New York*, 18 BUFF. L. REV. 393, 412-13 (1969). Seventy-four percent of the patients confined in Matteawan State Hospital on April 30, 1968, were patients in the incompetent to stand trial category. *Id.* at 413. See also Hess and Thomas, *Incompetency to Stand Trial: Procedures, Results and Problems*, 119 AM. J. PSYCHIATRY 713 (1963).

22. Comment, *Criminal Law—Insane Persons—Competency to Stand Trial*, 59 MICH. L. REV. 1078, 1088-89 (1961). *See also* Note, *Hospitalization of Mentally Ill Criminals in Pennsylvania and New Jersey*, 110 U. PA. L. REV. 78 (1961).

23. A. Matthews, *supra* note 20, at 193.

24. 406 U.S. 715 (1972).

25. *Id.* at 738 (footnote omitted).

26. *See, e.g.*, Bolton v. Harris, 295 F.2d 642 (D.C. Cir. 1968); State v. Clemons, 110 Ariz. 79, 515 P.2d 324 (1973); People v. Lally, 19 N.Y.2d 27, 224 N.E.2d 87, 277 N.Y.S.2d 654 (1966).

27. State v. Clemons, 110 Ariz. 79, 515 P.2d 324 (1973).

28. *See* discussion in text pp. 61-73 *infra*.

29. *See* discussion in text pp. 75-83 *infra*.

2 The Tests of Insanity

The M'Naghten or Right/Wrong Test

In the 1843 case of *Daniel M'Naghten*,[1] the House of Lords announced the following test of criminal responsibility:

> [T]o establish a defence on the ground of insanity, it must be clearly proved that, at the time of the committing of the act, the party accused was labouring under such a defect of reason, from disease of the mind, as not to know the nature and quality of the act he was doing; or, if he did know it, that he did not know he was doing what was wrong.[2]

Because it defines insanity solely in terms of impairment of *cognitive* capacity—that is, intellectual capacity to distinguish right from wrong—the *M'Naghten* test is the most restrictive test of criminal responsibility now used and has been severely criticized since first announced. As stated by one court, the thrust of the *M'Naghten* formulation is that ". . . there is a separate little man in the top of one's head called reason whose function it is to guide another unruly little man called instinct, emotion, or impulse in the way he should go."[3] The test reflects a traditional notion of a compartmentalized personality—a notion that is contrary to most psychiatrists' view of the personality as an integrated unit.[4] In 1953, the British Royal Commission on Capital Punishment summarized this criticism:

> [T]he M'Naghten Test is based on an entirely obsolete and misleading conception of the nature of insanity, since insanity does not only, or primarily, affect the cognitive or intellectual faculties, but affects the whole personality of the patient, including both the will and the emotions. An insane person may therefore often know the nature and quality of his act and that it is wrong and forbidden by law, but yet commit it as a result of the mental disease.[5]

Thus, critics assert that the *M'Naghten* test inadequately accounts for psychic realities and scientific knowledge and also fails in selecting all those not capable of making rational choices among alternative modes of behavior and who therefore should be absolved of criminal responsibility. Further, the *M'Naghten* test may unduly restrict psychiatric testimony and ask questions of a psychiatrist that he is unable to answer.[6]

Obvious ambiguities exist in the terminology of the *M'Naghten* test. Although the merits of *M'Naghten* have been debated extensively in legal literature, the key words of the test have rarely been construed in judicial opinions. For example, courts have almost never defined "disease of the mind," although the remainder of the test indicates that only the most severe mental conditions will qualify.

The use of the word *know* in *M'Naghten* has been subjected to scholarly criticism as referring to formal cognition or intellectual awareness alone; however, in most *M'Naghten* jurisdictions, *know* is not defined at all. The jury is simply given the words of the test, without explanation, and is thus permitted to adopt either a restrictive or a broad interpretation based on their own backgrounds and the evidence presented to them.[7] The appellate courts have generally approved a broad construction of the word.

> In eleven states, the jury is told that an accused "knows" only if he "understands" enough to enable him to judge of "the nature, character and consequence of the act charged against him," or if he has the "capacity to appreciate the character and to comprehend the probable or possible consequences of his act."[8]

Obviously, if the word *know* is broadly interpreted to include *both* intellectual *and* affective knowledge, so as to be in accord with modern psychiatric belief in an integrated personality, a major criticism of *M'Naghten* is invalidated.

In its original formulation, the *M'Naghten* test provides two criteria that must be met before the defendant is held criminally accountable. A defendant is not criminally responsible either if he does not know the nature and quality of the act or if he does not know the act is wrong. In using the test, many American jurisdictions phrase it solely in terms of the defendant's capacity to know right from wrong with respect to the criminal act committed. These jurisdictions seem to assume that the requirement of knowing "the nature and quality of the act" does not significantly add to the right/wrong test.

The Supreme Court of Wisconsin has rejected this assumption by holding that knowing "the nature and quality of the act" is significant in permitting a distinction to be made between vague realization "that particular conduct is forbidden" and "real insight into the conduct."[9] Arguably, a person might be able to retain intellectual knowledge of right and wrong and yet not understand the social significance of his conduct—that is, the nature and quality of his act.

Dean Goldstein has asserted:

> The broader reading of "nature and quality" carries with it the broader construction of "know" and vice versa. To know the quality of an act, with all its social and emotional implications, requires more than an abstract, purely intellectual knowledge. Likewise, to talk of appreciating the full significance of an act means that "nature and quality" must be understood as including more than the physical nature of the act.[10]

Thus, jurisdictions that equate knowledge of the nature and quality of the act with the ability to know the act is wrong may be applying an unduly restrictive *M'Naghten* test and may be unwittingly adding strength to the arguments of those who are dissatisfied with the test.

The word *wrong* in the *M'Naghten* test is also ambiguous. The language of the *M'Naghten* case itself indicates in one passage that "legal wrong" is the test[11] and in another passage that "moral wrong" is the test.[12] After one hundred and nine years, the English courts removed this ambiguity by ruling that to be criminally responsible, the accused must be aware the act was legally wrong.[13] In the United States, the word *wrong* is usually unexplained in jury instructions. In the few appellate cases where the issue has been raised, the courts have split. Where "moral wrong" is the standard chosen, an uncertainty remains whether the term ". . . is to be judged by the personal standards of the accused or by his awareness that society views the act as wrong."[14]

The Irresistible Impulse Test

No jurisdiction uses the irresistible impulse test as the sole standard of criminal responsibility; rather in those jurisdictions where it has been accepted, it is used in conjunction with and supplementary to the *M'Naghten* test. While *M'Naghten* by itself considers only the actor's cognition, the irresistible impulse addition permits examination of his volition (self-control). There is a recognition that mental illness may affect the actor's will and emotions as well as his cognitive or intellectual capacity. An individual is not criminally responsible under the irresistible impulse test if he had a mental disease that kept him from controlling his conduct, despite his knowledge of the nature and quality of his act and his awareness that it was wrong.

The major criticism of the irresistible impulse test comes from those who favor broadening *M'Naghten* to take into account the volitional element but who regard the irresisitible impulse test as inadequate in that it does not extend *M'Naghten* sufficiently. For example, Professor Herbert Wechsler objects to the concept of irresistibility because it requires a total impairment of volitional capacity.[15] The British Royal Commission on Capital Punishment rejected irresistible impulse because the word *impulse* implies that the defense is applicable only to those criminal acts which "have been suddenly and impulsively committed after a sharp internal conflict."[16] Chief Judge David Bazelon asserts that the irresistible impulse test gives ". . . no recognition to mental illness characterized by brooding and reflection and so relegates acts caused by such illness to the application of the inadequate right-wrong test."[17] The American Law Institute also views *impulse* as " . . . impliedly restricted to sudden spontaneous acts as distinguished from insane propulsions that are accompanied by brooding or reflection."[18]

This criticism has not gone unanswered. Dean Goldstein has pointed out that the phrase *irresistible impulse* is merely a textwriter's caption and is really not an appropriate title to describe the test in practice. "Most of the cases do not even use the phrase. It is much more accurate to describe the rules as concerned with lack of control and to use the shorthand designation 'control' test . . . ."[19] Because the jury is *not* told that proof of sudden, unplanned action is required for them to find loss of control,[20] a planned act may be sufficient to absolve a defendant of criminal liability.

Thus, the primary problem with the irresistible impulse test appears to be the often expressed but inaccurate belief that the test is interpreted narrowly. This problem leads some critics to the questionable conclusion that reform of the insanity defense requires adoption of a new test of criminal responsibility.

The Durham or Product Test

In *Durham v. United States*[21] decided in 1954, the Court of Appeals of the District of Columbia made an historic break from the *M'Naghten*-irresistible impulse formulations. Writing for the court, Judge Bazelon announced a new test[22] of criminal responsibility: "[A]n accused is not criminally responsible if his unlawful act was the product of mental disease or defect."[23]

The court premised its decision on the medically accepted view that because the mind functions as an integrated whole, the functions of cognition and control cannot be separated. Recognizing that an integrated personality cannot be only partially diseased, the court declared futile any attempt to identify types of malfunctioning symptoms:

> The question will be simply whether the accused acted because of a mental disorder, and not whether he displayed particular symptoms which medical science has long recognized do not necessarily, or even typically, accompany even the most serious mental disorder.[24]

In the court's view, the test would permit broadened expert testimony: psychiatrists would now be allowed to inform the jury of the character of the defendant's mental disease.

The *Durham* case unleashed a flood of commentary.[25] Psychiatrists generally favored the decision for "expand[ing] the area of inquiry and communication of the medical expert as a witness."[26] Lawyers, however, criticized *Durham* as being a non-rule. The test does not direct the jury to the pathological factors that are of concern to the law: impairment of reason and of control. "The jury was seemingly left entirely dependent upon the expert's classification of conduct as the 'product' of 'mental disease.'"[27] Additionally, these key terms are not defined in the *Durham* decision. For example, is "mental disease" purely a matter of psychiatric definition and determination, or may a court and jury decide contrary to psychiatric thought? If "mental disease," no matter how defined, has been found in an individual, may any act of the mentally ill person be termed a "product" of the illness? In other words, how great a causal connection must exist between the criminal act and the illness before the act is deemed a "product" of the illness?

Because the *Durham* decision announced a simple but ambiguous test, the District of Columbia court was forced to consider the substantive and procedural ramifications of its original position. In over one hundred appellate decisions following *Durham*, the court became a laboratory for resolution of issues that had long lain dormant. When *Durham* was decided, the court deliberately chose not to define the term "mental disease" so that expert testimony on the subject would be uninhibited. However, eight years later, the court expressed its concern that a medical definition of the term should not control the legal outcome of cases by constricting the scope of the jury's deliberations. In *McDonald v. United States*,[28] the court stated:

> [N]either the court nor the jury is bound by *ad hoc* definitions or conclusions as to what experts state is a disease or defect. . . . [T]he jury should be told that a mental disease or defect includes any abnormal condition of the mind which substantially affects mental or emotional processes and substantially impairs behavior controls. Thus the jury would consider testimony concerning the development, adaptation and functioning of these processes and controls.[29]

In *Carter v. United States*,[30] the court resolved an ambiguity concerning the word "product" in the *Durham* test. For the defense of insanity to be sucessfully asserted,

> [t]here must be a relationship between the disease and the act, and that relationship . . . must be . . . critical in its effect in respect to the act. By "critical" we mean decisive, determinative, causal; we mean to convey the idea inherent in the phrases "because of," "except for," "without which," "but for," "effect of," "result of," "causative factor"; the disease made the effective or decisive difference between doing and not doing the act. . . . [T]he facts concerning the disease and the facts concerning the act . . . [must be] such as to justify reasonably the conclusion that "But for this disease the act would not have been committed."[31]

Within a few years, Chief Justice Warren E. Burger, then a judge sitting on the District of Columbia Court of Appeals, expressed dissatisfaction with the "but for" clarification of *Carter*. As demonstrated by the following statement, he would construe the "product" requirement even more narrowly:

[A]ssuming arguendo that a criminal act can be the "product" of a "mental disease" that fact should not per se excuse the defendant; it should exculpate only if the condition described as a "mental disease" affected him so substantially that he could not appreciate the nature of the illegal act or could not control his conduct.[32]

This view may have been accepted indirectly with the *McDonald* definition of the term *mental disease*.

Although the *Durham* decision was applauded as broadening the scope of psychiatric testimony, *McDonald's* "mental disease" definition and *Carter's* "product" definition reflect the court's frustration with the way psychiatric testimony had been utilized. It is ironic, the court said, that

. . . the *Durham* rule, which was adopted in large part to permit experts to testify in their own terms concerning matters within their domain which the jury should know, resulted in testimony by the experts in terms not their own to reflect unexpressed judgments in a domain that is properly not theirs but the jury's. The irony is heightened when the jurymen, instructed under the esoteric "product" standard, are influenced significantly by "product" testimony of expert witnesses really reflecting ethical and legal judgments rather than a conclusion within the witnesses' particular expertise.[33]

The court's concern that experts were usurping the function of the jury culminated in *Washington v. United States*,[34] where the court stated:

The term "product" has no clinical significance for psychiatrists. Thus there is no justification for permitting psychiatrists to testify on the ultimate issue. Psychiatrists should explain how defendant's disease or defect relates to his alleged offense, that is, how the development, adaptation and functioning of defendant's behavioral processes may have influenced his conduct. But psychiatrists should not speak directly in terms of "product," or even "result" or "cause."[35]

Furthermore, in *Washington*, the court considered the propriety of psychiatrists testifying about whether defendant had a mental disease, for that determination is also part of the ultimate issue. Rather than prohibiting such testimony, the court published, in an appendix to its decision, an explanatory instruction to psychiatrists.[36] This instruction, given in open court prior to taking the testimony of the first psychiatric witness, explains that the clinical diagnostic meaning of "mental disease or defect" may be different from its legal meaning and that legal meaning is a question solely for the court and jury.

The American Law Institute's Model Penal Code Test

One year following the *Durham* decision, and prior to the *Carter, McDonald,* and *Washington* decisions clarifying the *Durham* test, the American Law Institute (hereinafter ALI) in its Model Penal Code, presented another formulation of the test of criminal responsibility. The ALI test now reads:[37]

> Section 4.01. Mental Disease or Defect Excluding Responsibility.
>
> (1)A person is not responsible for criminal conduct if at the time of such conduct as a result of mental disease or defect he lacks substantial capacity either to appreciate the criminality [wrongfulness] of his conduct or to conform his conduct to the requirements of law.
>
> (2)As used in this Article, the terms "mental disease or defect" do not include an abnormality manifested only by repeated criminal or otherwise anti-social conduct.[38]

Dean Goldstein explains the ALI test as follows:

> This test is a modernized and much improved rendition of *M'Naghten* and the "control" tests. It substitutes "appreciate" for "know," thereby indicating a preference for the view that a sane offender must be emotionally as well as intellectually aware of the significance of his conduct. And it uses the word "conform" instead of "control," while avoiding any reference to the misleading words "irresistible impulse." In addition, it requires only "substantial" incapacity, thereby eliminating the occasional references in the older cases to "complete" or "total" destruction of the normal capacity of the defendant.[39]

The ALI test has been hailed as a sensible compromise between the traditional tests and the radical-appearing *Durham* test.[40] In accepting the ALI test as the preferred formulation, the Fourth Circuit Court of Appeals stated:

> With appropriate balance between cognition and volition, it demands an unrestricted inquiry into the whole personality of a defendant . . . . Its verbiage is unerstandable by psychiatrists; it imposes no limitation upon their testimony, and yet, to a substantial extent, it avoids a diagnostic approach and leaves the jury free to make its findings in terms of a standard which society prescribes and juries may apply.[41]

However, critics contend that important words in the ALI test—for example, "substantial" and "appreciate"—are vague and undefined. Judge Bazelon recently opined that the difficulties the court faced with the word "product" in the *Durham* test may be repeated with the word "result" in the ALI test. He warns against ". . . the articulation of a catchphrase that facilitates conclusory expert testimony and that obscures the moral and legal overtones of the productivity question."[42] Judge Bazelon has also criticized the ALI formulation for continuing to require that the accused have a "mental disease" as a prerequisite condition of non-responsibility. His view is that the term is too entangled with the medical model—that is, mental disorder explained as an illness—to be usable as a legal concept:

If a defendant is prepared to present evidence that his mental or emotional processes and behavior controls were in fact impaired, it is not clear why anything should turn on the experts' view of his condition in the abstract.[43]

Judge Bazelon also noted that ". . . the validity of the 'medical model' is seriously questioned by some eminent psychiatrists."[44]

Paragraph (2) of the ALI test attempts to exclude psychopathic personality disorders from the definition of "mental disease or defect." Thus, psychopaths would be held criminally responsible. The comments to this paragraph justify such exclusion as follows:

While it may not be feasible to formulate a definition of "disease," there is much to be said for excluding a condition that is manifested only by the behavior phenomena that must, by hypothesis, be the result of disease for irresponsibility to be established.[45]

The strongest criticism of the ALI test has been addressed to paragraph (2). Some critics oppose a rigid rule excluding psychopaths because of existing doubts about whether the psychopathic personality is a valid psychiatric classification.[46] For example, Dr. Bernard Diamond has asserted:

[R]estrictive clauses aimed at excluding certain specified categories of individuals from exculpation simply do not make any psychiatric sense. They are as arbitrary and capricious as excluding defendants with red hair or blue eyes or Negro blood from the benefits of the law of criminal responsibility. They define by legislative fiat what is and what is not a psychiatric condition.[47]

Other critics contend that psychopathy is never manifested solely by repeated criminal conduct[48] and that therefore any effort to exclude psychopaths from the insanity defense based on paragraph (2) must fail.

The Justly Responsible Test

In 1953, the Royal Commission on Capital Punishment proposed that a person should not be criminally responsible for his unlawful act if ". . . at the time of the act the accused was suffering from disease of the mind (or mental deficiency) to such a degree that he ought not to be held responsible."[49] That proposal has not become law in Great Britain. Professor Herbert Wechsler, Reporter for the ALI's Model Penal Code, recommended a modified version of this test in 1955. That proposal, which appears as an alternative formulation of the ALI test in its 1955 tentative draft report,[50] was not accepted by a majority of the ALI's Council. Recently, Judge Bazelon has become an advocate of this approach, which is referred to as the justly responsible test. He concurs with those who assert that the *Durham* formulation should be abandoned, and he would phrase the test this way:

[A] defendant is not responsible if at the time of his unlawful conduct his mental or emotional processes or behavior controls were impaired to such an extent that he cannot justly be held responsible for his act.[51]

Judge Bazelon's change of mind, only eighteen years after he authored the *Durham* decision and in the face of Great Britain's rejection of the Royal Commission's proposal and the ALI's rejection of a similar proposal by its own Reporter, is indeed remarkable. Judge Bazelon explains the reasons for his change as follows:

Durham reformulated the responsibility test in the hope that new and more useful information would be presented to the jury. We acted largely in response to the plea of behavioral scientists that they did not want to decide ultimate questions of law and morality, but wanted only an opportunity to report their findings as scientific investigators without the need to force their findings through the prism of M'Naghten. . . . But it quickly became apparent that while our decision produced some expansion of the inquiry, it did not do nearly enough to eliminate the experts' stranglehold on the process. . . . [T]he experts continued, on the whole, to speak in conclusory terms which inevitably included but concealed their underlying value judgments, and their own views as to the appropriate legal outcome.[52]

He noted also that even after the court's decision in *Washington v. United States*, psychiatrists ". . . continued to make moral and legal judgments beyond the proper scope of their professional expertise."[53]

Judge Bazelon believes that the justly responsible test he now propounds will eliminate encroachments by the experts on the jury's function of intertwining moral, legal, and medical considerations on which the resolution of the responsibility question properly depends. His formulation of the justly responsible test

. . . would ask the psychiatrist a single question: what is the nature of the impairment of the defendant's mental and emotional processes and behavior controls? It would leave for the jury the question whether that impairment is sufficient to relieve the defendant of responsibility for the particular act charged.[54]

The justly responsible approach has been criticized since it was announced by the Royal Commission. Three dissenting Commission members considered it a non-test that exposes defendants to unlimited arbitrariness of jurors. They contended that juries would not be guided in deciding among opinions of expert witnesses and that uniformity in decision making would thus be sacrificed.[55] The majority of the Court of Appeals of the District of Columbia, in rejecting a justly responsible formulation, stated:

It is one thing . . . to tolerate and even welcome the jury's sense of equity as a force that affects its application of instructions which state the legal rules that crystallize the requirements of justice as determined by the lawmakers of the community. It is quite another to set the jury at large, without such crystallization, to evolve its own legal rules and standards of justice.[56]

Acting through courts and legislatures, society decides the basic moral issues of responsibility and in so doing determines the test of blameworthiness.[57] The jury's function is to apply this test to a particular individual in a particular set of circumstances. As one author notes:

[T]he jurors are the arbiters of the facts, not of the law. . . . To say that jurors would determine criminal irresponsibility on the basis of whether defendant is blameworthy is to say they would make their determination on the basis of what each thinks the law is . . . .[58]

The justly responsible test has also been attacked for the heavy burden it places on the jury. Without any guidance, jurors are expected to determine responsibility on the basis of their own personal feelings about the defendant. Juries that are instructed under a more definitive insanity test imposed on them by a court or legislature are able to rationalize their verdicts as "required," and thus they have an easier task.[59]

Reconciliation of the Insanity Tests

It is important to ask whether a significant difference exists among the various insanity tests both in language and in practical application. The American Bar Foundation has suggested that the ALI test is little more than a modernized combination of *M'Naghten* and irresistible impulse. Similarly, the *Durham* test as clarified by the *McDonald* case does not differ substantially from the ALI formulation. Thus, the following equation would seem appropriate: *M'Naghten* plus irresistible impulse equals ALI, equals *Durham* plus *McDonald*.[60]

Much of the controversy over the relative desirability of the respective rules would then seem superfluous. However, such logic may be viewed as too simplistic to be acceptable. One would expect the differences in nuance and emphasis, explicit references to scope and conclusiveness of expert testimony, and varying standards of cognition and volition to have some impact of greater than mere artistic appreciability.[61]

The major criticism of *M'Naghten* is that the test restricts psychiatric testimony, thereby denying the jury modern psychological insights that may present a fuller picture of the defendant's mental condition. But Dean Goldstein has critiqued the critics, charging that their position is unsupported either by court decisions or by authorities on the law of evidence.

When the insanity defense is being tried, courts in *M'Naghten* jurisdictions usually admit all probative evidence of the defendant's mental condition. Testimony regarding defendant's deviant behavior is not excluded simply because it does not fit the narrow cognition boundary of the *M'Naghten* test, which is applied at the end of the trial.[62]

A field study conducted by the American Bar Foundation in five states and the District of Columbia supports Dean Goldstein's observation that in actual practice *M'Naghten* does not inhibit expert testimony at the trial level:

> We have not found psychiatric testimony excluded or even seriously limited under *M'Naghten* except where witnesses were clearly rambling or where testimony was irrelevant in a commonsensical view of legal relevancy. Expert witnesses are able and encouraged to state background information and medical opinions. None of the many officials we interviewed—psychiatrists, defense and prosecuting attorneys, and judges who had taken part in many cases over the years—could recall an example of a case in which psychiatric testimony was seriously restricted. Particularly in capital cases, judges will err on the side of admitting defense evidence unless it is clearly prejudicial or repetitive.[63]

Moreover, when the issue has been raised on appeal, courts have generally affirmed the propriety of unrestricted expert testimony.[64] For example, one state supreme court has noted:

> To resolve this vital issue of criminal responsibility it is necessary that the jury have the entire picture of the defendant. Insanity resulting in criminal acts is not a sudden growth even if the prohibited conduct seems to be of a sudden explosive nature. . . . [I]t is always permissible, when searching for the real cause "to show previous troubles" if it throws light on the act constituting the crime or explains the reason for its commission.[65]

This court added that without complete explanation the jury would be allowed to hear only the psychiatrist's conclusion. The psychiatrist should relate, in language understandable to the layperson, the defendant's case history so that the jury may properly evaluate the bases of this conclusion.[66]

If *M'Naghten* does not preclude a presentation to the jury of all facets of the defendant's mental condition, what then is the test's shortcoming? Dean Goldstein suggests that the answer lies in the preconceptions of the criminal trial's participants. Lawyers and psychiatrists in *M'Naghten* jurisdictions present their evidence as if the defense is to be narrowly construed. They assume, for example, that the psychiatrist is ". . . required to testify in terms of a definition of 'know' which is limited to formal cognition and excludes any emotional appreciation of the act and its consequences."[67] They equate insanity with psychosis, thereby excluding "lesser" mental illnesses. Thus, the defense is unnecessarily restricted to a small group of totally deteriorated psychotics.[68] In short, the fault of *M'Naghten* "lies less with the formulation of the defense than with its presentation."[69]

Trial courts in *M'Naghten* jurisdictions may be confused about the admissibility of broad psychiatric evidence. Two of the three cases Dean Goldstein utilizes to illustrate the point that psychiatric testimony is not inhibited by *M'Naghten* are cases in which the trial court rejected psychiatric testimony as not probative. One case involved a medical witness attempting to testify that the defendant could not control his behavior (that is, irresistible impulse);[70] the other involved an effort to prove the defendant was a psychopath.[71] The trial court errors in unduly restricting psychiatric testimony were corrected only through the appellate process.

Dean Goldstein suggests that psychiatrists' and trial lawyers' misconceptions about the irresistible impulse test, not the formulation of the test itself, inhibit psychiatrists' testimony and even cause lawyers' decisions not to plead the defense at all.

> [T]he criticism to which the "control" tests have been subjected may result in their value being underestimated and their use neglected. As in the case of *M'Naghten*, lawyers and psychiatrists may fail to see cases as appropriate for the defense, in reliance upon criteria imposed upon them by no court or legislature.[72]

Finally, at least one noted jurist has taken exception to Dean Goldstein's contention that psychiatric testimony has seldom been limited in practice by narrow judicial application of the *M'Naghten* and irresistible impulse tests. Judge Bazelon has maintained that in the District of Columbia, prior to the 1954 adoption of the *Durham* test, ". . . the traditional rules were regularly applied to prevent psychiatrists from explaining their insights in broad terms."[73]

The data on psychiatric testimony suggest that although *M'Naghten* plus irresistible impulse could be construed broadly enough to conform, at least roughly, to ALI and to *Durham* plus *McDonald*, the test is currently not so broadly construed by participants in a criminal trial.

The determination of whether the various insanity tests are reconcilable requires examining the outcome of similar cases to see if application of one test leads to conviction while application of another leads to an insanity acquittal. Unfortunately, as reported by the American Bar Foundation, adequate data are not available, conclusions that can be derived from available data are inconsistent, and a question of validity remains even if the problem of reliability can be overcome.[74] Nevertheless, through brief examination of available statistics, speculation is possible on the reasons that reliable inferences can not be drawn.

The impact of the *Durham* decision on the results of District of Columbia criminal cases has been reported in several studies. One study shows that from 1953 (when the test of responsibility in the District was *M'Naghten* plus irresistible impulse) to 1961 (seven years after the *Durham* test went into effect), acquittals by reason of insanity rose from less than 1 percent to more than 14 percent.[75] Another study shows that insanity acquittals in the District were between 0.2 percent and 0.6 percent in the three years immediately preceding the *Durham* decision, rose to 1 percent in the three years succeeding *Durham*, and were 6 percent in 1961 (seven years after *Durham* was announced).[76] This study notes that the increase in insanity verdicts ". . . took place at the expense of the acquittals [verdicts of not guilty] and not at the expense of the guilty verdicts."[77] The President's Commission on Crime in the District of Columbia found that since the 1962 *McDonald* decision clarifying *Durham*, "insanity acquittals have stabilized at two to three percent of all defendants."[78] The District of Columbia Court of Appeals updated the Commission's report and found that insanity acquittals have run at about 2 percent of all cases terminated since *McDonald*. Further, the court found that during the seven-year period following *McDonald* (1962-1969), juries found only twenty-one defendants not guilty by reason of insanity.[79]

The above-cited statistics do not seem to demonstrate that a shift from a "restrictive" *M'Naghten* test to a "liberal" *Durham* test causes significant change overall in case results. And even the slight increase in percent of insanity acquittals is not necessarily attributable solely to the change in insanity test formulation. The American Bar Foundation lists several other factors that may have affected the results of District of Columbia cases. For example, (1) the burden of proof is favorable to the accused; (2) the District of Columbia bar is relatively sophisticated about mental illness due to the controversy following the *Durham* decision; (3) the jury is informed that acquittal of the defendant on grounds of insanity entails commitment to St. Elizabeths Hospital; and (4) the racial composition of the District, with a high proportion of Black jurors and Black defendants, may make juries favorably disposed to a defense plea of insanity.[80]

Studies using mock juries have attempted to ascertain the practical impact of various insanity formulations. In one experiment, sociologist Rita Simon studied responses of 1,176 jurors from jury pools in three large cities.[81] Juries listened to the same recorded trials. Then each received instructions based on either the *M'Naghten* formulation, the *Durham* formulation, or the following "non-test" instruction: "If you believe that the defendant was insane at the time he committed the acts of which he is accused, then you must find the accused not guilty by reason of insanity."[82] The *Durham*-instructed juries returned insanity verdicts in somewhat more cases than the *M'Naghten*-instructed juries. The "non-test"-instructed juries returned insanity verdicts in slightly more instances than the *Durham*-instructed juries. Simon concludes ". . . that the criterion for criminal responsibility as defined under *Durham* is closer to the jury's natural sense of equity than is the *M'Naghten* rule.''[83]

Another important finding of the study is that jurors can not distinguish among the various insanity tests as presented to them in a brief jury instruction. The researcher states: ''The practical implications suggested are that differences between *M'Naghten* and *Durham* may be too subtle to be fully grasped . . . .''[84]

Other studies support this disturbing conclusion. In one, ten mock juries selected from Chicago jury pools listened to a criminal trial involving the insanity defense. The juries' deliberations were transcribed and analyzed. This researcher reports that jurors spent only 8 percent of their time on the court's instructions and that they were only 58 percent accurate in recalling these instructions. This was the lowest accuracy recall rate of any material heard during the trial.[85]

In another study, 229 volunteer college students in District of Columbia universities listened to jury instructions based on *Durham* and were then immediately tested for comprehension. The test questions were ''deliberately couched in the legal language of the jury charges in order to stimulate recall.''[86] Nevertheless, ''[i]n three out of four trials, only one-third of the jurors could be expected to recall the judge's charges with significant accuracy during deliberations on the law of insanity.''[87] A characteristic response of those erroneously describing the *Durham* test requirements is: ''He [defendant] must be completely unreasonable, incapable of thinking.''[88]

These studies have been interpreted to mean

> . . . that the jury (1) does not understand the code of the psychiatrist, (2) does not understand the legal framework, and (3) applies its own reasoning to the case to the extent of regarding its own fears as more important than the elaborate judicial system. In other words, the layman, the juror, puts his own ''value'' on the asocial behavior.[89]

An author concludes that one solution to the problem is to vest the judgment of criminal responsibility in a panel of experts rather than in the jury.[90]

I believe this conclusion is totally without merit. Despite evidence indicating deficiencies in the jury's understanding, the jury is the representative of society that should determine the point at which mental disorder should absolve an individual from criminal responsibility. No panel of experts can properly determine that point, for ''. . . the evaluation of the defendant's impairment in light of community standards of blameworthiness . . . is the very essence of the jury's role.''[91]

The consideration of whether the various insanity tests are reconcilable must take into account the community's willingness to accept mental illness as a condition excusing criminal responsibility. Jury verdicts are a measure of this acceptance. Dean Goldstein notes:

> Jurors find it difficult to accept the idea of serious mental disorder unless it is accompanied by visible and gross psychotic symptoms—either a breakdown in intellect or the loss of self-control. In this respect, they share the reluctance of most people to concede that persons who seem very much like themselves may be seriously ill. . . . [P]ublic attitudes regarding crime and mental illness limit the practical utility of the insanity defense, in whatever form it may be cast and however freely evidence may be admitted.[92]

Recommendation

A strong argument can be made for legislative inaction—that is, a legislative refusal to enact any specific insanity test. Dr. Bernard Diamond has stated that the problems of the mentally ill offender "are not soluble through manipulation of the legal rules of responsibility."[93] The law's quest for certainty cannot be achieved through adoption of a test that broadens psychiatric testimony concerning mental illness. Paradoxically, the advances of scientific knowledge about mental illness have resulted in confusion and uncertainty regarding some of psychiatry's most basic tenets. Thus, "[t]he psychiatry of the 1970's is well advanced over that of the 1950's, but it is less usable by the law."[94] When the District of Columbia Court of Appeals recently reconsidered its decision in the *Durham* case, Judge Bazelon noted:

> This Court's search for a new set of words to define the elusive concept of responsibility has a distinctly archaic quality. The arguments for and against the *Durham* wording, the wording of the majority and minority versions of the ALI test, and the wording of *McDonald,* were clearly articulated many years ago. What should by now be clear is that the problems of the responsibility defense cannot be resolved by adopting for the standard or the jury instruction any new formulation of words. The practical operation of the defense is primarily controlled by other factors . . . . [W]e cannot allow our search for the perfect choice of words to deflect our attention from the far more important practical questions. For it is on those questions that the rationality and fairness of the responsibility defense will ultimately turn.[95]

I concur with Dr. Diamond's and Judge Bazelon's judgment that the problems of criminal responsibility cannot be resolved by adopting any particular insanity test. I also agree that concern over semantics should not preclude examination of other insanity defense issues. Clearly an ultimate or perfect test of criminal responsibility is impossible. However, despite these limitations, there are reasons for proposing legislative action to formulate a test of criminal responsibility. The American Bar Foundation asserts:

> Granting that the "modern" tests of criminal responsibility indeed fail to lead to a socio-legal "promised land," the problem with such observations is that they often become the parlance of those who are unwilling to advocate or even entertain the thought of any "real change" in our conceptions and institutions such as might bring the criminal justice system closer to ideals of consistency and rationality, and tend to justify the principle of inertia, espousing old rules and formulations by default.[96]

Courts are faced with critical decisions affecting the lives of criminal defendants. Those decisions must be made today: They cannot await an indefinite future time when a standard for personal blameworthiness might be scientifically established.[97] Any legislative judgment improving the administration of criminal justice, even to a minor degree, is warranted now.

The material in the previous section of this book suggests that the various tests overlap to a great extent and that even the most liberal test is not likely to alter significantly jury decision making on criminal responsibility. However this does not mean that the tests are identical or that a jury's judgment in an individual case will not be affected by the jurisdiction's insanity test. For example, Dean Goldstein strongly advocates the position that *M'Naghten* can be construed more broadly than it currently is. Nevertheless, even he admits that the *M'Naghten* formulation cannot be expanded to include the concept that impaired control should result in an insanity acquittal.[98]

Finally, a legislative failure to act constitutes action by default to continue whichever test now exists in the state. Particularly in those jurisdictions where the test has been court imposed, legislative judgment may be desirable, for broad policy decisions are more appropriately in the domain of the legislature.

Appendix A-1 lists each state's test of insanity. *M'Naghten*, currently the most widely used test, is the choice in twenty-one states. Eleven states use a combination of *M'Naghten* plus irresistible impulse. Only two employ *Durham*, and seventeen use the ALI test. Additionally, ten of the eleven federal judicial circuits have accepted either the ALI test itself or a modified version thereof. The court of appeals in the remaining federal circuit has yet to reconsider the insanity test issue, but it has commended to the attention of trial courts in its circuit the ALI test.[99]

There is a definite trend toward acceptance of the ALI test. In California, an influential state that still adheres to *M'Naghten*, one supreme court justice, relying partly on the almost uniform acceptance of the ALI test in the federal circuits, has advocated a switch to ALI.[100]

The trend toward ALI will no doubt be accelerated by the recent decision of the prestigious Court of Appeals of the District of Columbia in *United States v. Brawner*.[101] The court, sitting en banc, considered the *Brawner* case for more than a year. At the request of the court, briefs amicus curiae were filed by the following groups: American Civil Liberties Union, American Psychiatric Association, American Psychological Association, National District Attorneys Association, National Legal Aid and Defender Association, Public Defenders Service, and the Bar Association of the District of Columbia. Amici briefs were also filed by Professor David L. Chambers, III, of the University of Michigan School of Law and Mr. William H. Dempsey, Jr., who was specially appointed by the court as amicus.[102] The court thoroughly reconsidered the insanity test and in an exhaustive opinion[103] abandoned *Durham* and adopted ALI. The court stated:

> The American Law Institute's Model Penal Code expressed a rule which has become the dominant force in the law pertaining to the defense of insanity. The ALI rule is eclectic in spirit, partaking of the moral focus of *M'Naghten*, the practical accommodation of the "control rules" [that is, irresistible impulse] . . . , and responsive, at the same time, to a relatively modern, forward-looking view of what is encompassed in "knowledge."[104]

Even before the *Brawner* decision, Dean Goldstein maintained that ALI will "undoubtedly gain even wider acceptance"[105] because it is viewed as a sensible compromise between extreme positions. He summarizes this point as follows:

> The new rules which appeared on the scene in the 1950s represented a flight from law. They swung from the extreme of abandoning the effort to frame a legal standard [that is, abolition of the insanity defense], giving the matter entirely to the jury [that is, the justly responsible test], to the opposite extreme of trying to give the matter almost entirely to the psychiatrists [that is, the unmodified *Durham* test]. The first never won favor; the second has seen the medical-seeming standard shaped by an adversary system into something as much legal as medical. In reaction against both extremes, the American Law Institute resumed the effort to frame a standard which joins medical science and social purpose. Its proposal solves most of the problems generally associated with the older rules while at the same time representing the same line of historical development. As a result, it is likely to become the formula for the immediate future in the United States.[106]

I recommend that the legislature adopt the following test of criminal responsibility:

> *A person is not criminally responsible for his conduct if, as a result of impairment of his mental or emotional processes or behavior controls, he lacked, at the time of such conduct, substantial capacity either to appreciate the wrongfulness of his conduct or to conform his conduct to the requirements of law.*

Explanation of Word Choice in the Recommendation

The statute I recommend is a modified formulation of the ALI test. The words were chosen deliberately and deserve explanation.

First, the ALI test begins with the statement that: "A person is not responsible for *criminal conduct* if at the time of such *conduct* . . ." (emphasis added). Because the insanity test absolves the defendant from criminal responsibility, it may be a non sequitur to label his conduct "criminal conduct." For conduct to be "criminal conduct," the defendant must do more than perform an act that would be criminal if he possessed the requisite *mens rea*: He must actually have that *mens rea* at the time he acted. To avoid this technical inconsistency in the ALI test, I recommend substituting the following words: *"A person is not criminally responsible for his conduct if . . . at the time of such conduct . . . ."*[107]

Second, the ALI test is phrased in medical model terminology: " . . . as a result of mental disease or defect . . . ." As discussed previously,[108] judges are becoming increasingly concerned that the legal determination of insanity, supposedly made by the jury, is in fact made by the psychiatrist through his medical determination of mental illness. Judge Bazelon states:

> Too often a defendant's responsibility seems to turn on whether or not the experts have given his condition a name and the status of an "illness." It seems to me that the label "mental illness" impedes understanding rather than advancing it. There is no reason to tie the legal concept of responsibility to the medical model of mental illness, especially when the validity of that medical model is seriously questioned by some eminent psychiatrists. . . .
>
> In order to be sure that the jury does not defer to the expert's decision on the matter of mental illness, it may well be appropriate to abandon the term "mental illness" altogether.[109]

Moreover, deference to psychiatric judgment is unwise for psychiatrists themselves do not agree on what constitutes mental illness. As one noted forensic psychiatrist explains:

> The second edition of the *Diagnostic and Statistical Manual*, which is the standard for American psychiatric nomenclature, tries to be comprehensive and provide a diagnostic label to fit anyone a psychiatrist might ever see in his office. This is very convenient for filling out insurance forms on patients who are not really sick but just have problems.
>
> But real disputes arise in sanity determinations over the question of whether a particular diagnosis is or is not a "mental disease." As a general rule a court will accept a diagnosis as a "mental disease" if the expert witness says it is. But psychiatrists do not agree at all among themselves as to which of these diagnoses are diseases. Psychiatrists are even less in agreement as to the general definition of what constitutes mental disease, although many psychiatric theorists have opinions on this point. But it sometimes happens in a trial that the psychiatrists agree on the

defendant's symptoms and diagnosis, but they disagree as to whether the diagnosis in question is a mental illness. Such cases are not rare, and they would be far more frequent if every defendant were examined by more than one psychiatrist.[110]

In the *Brawner* decision, the Court of Appeals for the District of Columbia engrafted on to the ALI test the non-medical definition of "mental disease or defect" that that court had announced previously in the *McDonald* decision.[111] The court expressed the view that such an approach would sanction expert testimony "while guarding against the undue dominance of expert testimony or specialized labels."[112]

However, Judge Bazelon criticized the court's "ALI plus *McDonald*" solution as leaving ". . . the power of the experts intact. Expert witnesses still testify in misleading and conclusory terms about the medical or psychiatric definitions of mental disease."[113]

The difficulties encountered by the *McDonald* approach that retains the medical model of mental disease but also attempts to clarify that term by declaring it a legal concept is illustrated by examining a specific diagnosis. For example, is heroin addiction a "mental disease"? A psychiatrist notes:

It is the only psychiatric disease that has as one of its typical manifestations an irresistible compulsion to commit crimes. It is the only psychiatric disease in which the impairment of behavior control can be measured: less than five percent of addicts who have been withdrawn and returned to the community are able to avoid readdiction within a year. Voluntary withdrawal from heroin by persons with access to the drug is virtually unknown. Although the disease has little effect on cognitive processes, there is no psychiatric disease that has a greater effect on emotional processes. But in spite of all this, the United States Court of Appeals for the District of Columbia has refused to rule that heroin addiction is a mental disease that could constitute a basis for the insanity defense under . . . *McDonald*. Each time the court makes a new ruling on this point, the opinion becomes more lengthy, obscure, and the reasoning of the court appears more tortuous and artificial.[114]

I recommend substituting for the ALI language the following words: ". . . *if, as a result of impairment of his mental or emotional processes or behavior controls* . . . ." This proposal to eliminate the medical model will permit a jury to consider impairment arising from physiological, emotional, social, or cultural sources.[115] Some might argue that this change is revolutionary and expands the test into unknown territory. However, the proposed language is governed by the remainder of the ALI test, which focuses the jury's attention on the *extent* to which the impairment has affected the defendant's cognitive and volitional capacities. I have rejected the more radical justly responsible formulation, which does not contain this governing factor. The language I propose will still permit psychiatrists to testify on the accused's mental condition using their own nomenclature. However, the proposed language, together with trial court instructions, should aid the jury in understanding that its determination on criminal responsibility involves more than blind acceptance of psychiatric testimony that the defendant was or was not mentally diseased. Therefore, though significant, the proposed change is evolutionary.

Third, the ALI test contains this language: " . . . either to appreciate the criminality [wrongfulness] of his conduct . . . ." Aside from choosing between the words "criminality" and "wrongfulness" (to be discussed below), I recommend language that does not depart from this portion of the ALI formulation. In *United States v. Currens*,[116] the United States Court of Appeals for the Third Circuit adopted the ALI test but eliminated the above-quoted language. Judge Biggs, writing for the majority, stated:

> We are unable to accept the phrase "to appreciate the criminality of his conduct." This phrase would overemphasize the cognitive element in criminal responsibility and thus distract the jury from the crucial issues while being little more than surplusage.[117]

Defenders of the *Currens* formulation contend that the appropriate legal issue to be determined is whether the individual was substantially able to conform his conduct to the law's requirements. This issue cannot be resolved by focusing on the defendant's cognitive capacity, which is just one particular facet of his integrated personality. Cognitive impairment is important only when it substantially incapacitates volitional function.[118]

Most courts have refused to treat the knowledge feature as merely one aspect of the ultimate control element and thus have rejected the *Currens* formulation.[119] Although these courts admit that the *Currens* position may be theoretically defensible, they assert that a pragmatic justification exists for retaining the language of cognition. In the determination of criminal responsibility, the law is concerned with the morality of conduct. Instructing the jury on the cognitive element as part of the test of criminal responsibility reenforces the societal judgment that a person who cannot appreciate the wrongfulness of his act should not be punished as a criminal, for he is not morally blameworthy.

As stated in the *Brawner* decision:

> [W]e resist the *Currens* lure of logic in order to make certain that the jury will give heed to the substantiality of a defense of lack of substantial capacity to appreciate wrongfulness, a point that may elude a jury instructed solely in terms of control capacity.[120]

Fourth, the ALI test permits a choice between the words "criminality" and "wrongfulness." I have chosen "*wrongfulness*" as the preferable word for several reasons. First, *M'Naghten* alone or *M'Naghten* plus irresistible impulse is presently applied in thirty-two states; this test uses the word "wrong" (see Appendix A-1). Additionally, twelve of the seventeen states and eight of the ten federal circuits that have adopted ALI use "wrongfulness." Thus, a jury instruction under my formulation would be similar to the instruction currently given to juries in most jurisdictions. Second, "wrongfulness" has been chosen by the most influential jurisdictions, including the District of Columbia Court of Appeals in *Brawner*.[121] Third, legal authorities have favored the word "wrongfulness." For example, Professor Henry Weihofen noted that if the word "criminality" is used, society will ". . . condemn as responsible and fit for punishment some of the most wildly disordered persons ever seen . . . ."[122]

Fifth, I reject paragraph (2) of the ALI test. A previous portion of this book discusses the criticism of the paragraph for its attempt to preclude exculpation of sociopaths.[123] A federal court[124] expands on this criticism by basing its refusal to accept the paragraph on three grounds. First, the language of paragraph (2) would be ineffectual in excluding sociopaths; it is always possible to introduce some evidence, other than past criminal behavior, to support a plea of insanity. Second, if paragraph (2) is adopted, society will receive insufficient protection from potential recidivists, for sociopaths convicted of crimes are released after a fixed period of years. If paragraph (2) is rejected and the insanity defense is available, sociopaths are more likely to be indefinitely committed following acquittal. Third,

> [i]t would be reason enough for us to refuse to approve § 4.01 (2) on the grounds that if fails to accomplish the only purpose, one of debatable value, for which it was intended, and that it would burden trial courts and juries with an extra instruction which should have little, if any, impact on any necessary factual determination. There is, however, additional cause for our concern. This is the paragraph's ambiguity. It is unclear whether § 4.01 (2) would require that a defendant be considered legally sane if, although the only overt acts manifesting his disease or defect were "criminal or otherwise anti-social," there arises from his acts a reasonable inference of mental derangement either because of the nature of the acts or because of credible medical or other evidence. Since § 4.01 (2) is ambiguous to us, it is reasonable to believe that an instruction incorporating the section would be equally confusing and ambiguous to jurors.[125]

Do sociopaths fit the definition of persons who should be found criminally irresponsible? In my opinion there is as yet no answer to this question. With the current state of psychiatric knowledge—or lack thereof—the law should not presume to give a definitive answer. Each case should be handled on an individual basis—that is, depending on the psychiatric and lay testimony heard by the jury, some sociopaths may be found guilty and some may be acquitted by reason of insanity.

Notes

1. M'Naghten's Case, 10 Clark & Fin. 200, 8 Eng. Rep. 718 (1843).

2. *Id*. at 210, 8 Eng. Rep. at 722.

3. Holloway v. United States, 148 F.2d 665, 667 (D.C. Cir. 1945), *cert. denied*, 334 U.S. 852 (1948).

4. Hall, *Psychiatry and Criminal Responsibility*, 65 YALE L.J. 761, 775 (1956).

5. Royal Commission on Capital Punishment 1949-53, REPORT 80 (London: Her Majesty's Stationery Office, 1953).

6. American Bar Foundation, THE MENTALLY DISABLED AND THE LAW 386-87, rev. ed., Brakel and Rock, eds. (Chicago: University of Chicago Press, 1971). *But see* W. LaFave and A. Scott, HANDBOOK ON CRIMINAL LAW 282 (St. Paul: West Publishing Co., 1972).

7. A. Goldstein, THE INSANITY DEFENSE 50 (New Haven: Yale University Press, 1967).

8. *Id*. at 49-50.

9. State v. Esser, 16 Wis. 2d 567, 115 N.W.2d 505, 521 (1962).

10. A Goldstein, *supra* note 7, at 51.

11. M'Naghten's Case, 10 Clark & Fin. 200, 209, 8 Enq. Rep. 718, 722 (1843).

12. *Id*. at 210-11, 8 Eng. Rep. at 723.

13. Regina v. Windle, [1952] 2 Q.B. 826, 2 All E.R. 1.

14. A. Goldstein, *supra* note 7, at 52.

15. Wechsler, *The Criteria of Criminal Responsibility*, 22 U. CHI. L. REV. 367, 375 (1955).

16. Royal Commission on Capital Punishment, *supra* note 5 at 110.

17. Durham v. United States, 214 F.2d 862, 873-74 (D.C. Cir. 1954).

18. MODEL PENAL CODE § 4.01, Comments, at 157 (Tent. Draft No. 4, 1955).

19. A. Goldstein, *supra* note 7, at 69.

20. *Id*. at 71-73.

21. 214 F.2d 862 (D.C. Cir. 1954).

22. Actually, the *Durham* rule is a reiteration of the New Hampshire rule announced by the supreme court of that state in State v. Jones, 50 N.H. 369 (1871).

23. Durham v. United States, 214 F.2d 862, 874-75 (D.C. Cir. 1954) (footnote omitted).

24. *Id*. at 876 (footnote omitted).

25. W. LaFave and A. Scott, *supra* note 6, at 288 n.16 lists a "representative sampling" of sixteen articles written about the *Durham* decision.

26. Roche, *Criminality and Mental Illness–Two Faces of the Same Coin*, 22 U. CHI. L. REV. 320, 324 (1955).

27. A. Goldstein, *supra* note 7, at 84.

28. 312 F.2d 847 (D.C. Cir. 1962).

29. *Id*. at 851.

30. 252 F.2d 608 (D.C. Cir. 1957).

31. *Id*. at 617.

32. Blocker v. United States, 288 F.2d 853, 862 (D.C. Cir. 1961) (Burger, J., concurring in the result only) (footnote omitted).

33. United States v. Brawner, 471 F.2d 969, 983 (D.C. Cir. 1972).

34. 390 F.2d 444 (D.C. Cir. 1967).

35. *Id*. at 456.

36. *Id*. at 457-58.

37. The 1962 Proposed Official Draft differs from the 1955 Tentative Draft in two respects: (1) the bracketed word "wrongfulness" was inserted in the final draft to indicate an option in word choice; and (2) the words "As used in this Article" were added to the final draft to clarify that the section is not attempting to legislate medical terminology.

38. MODEL PENAL CODE § 4.01 (Proposed Official Draft 1962).

39. A. Goldstein, *supra* note 7, at 87.

40. *See id*. at 93.

41. United States v. Chandler, 393 F.2d 920, 926 (4th Cir. 1968) (footnotes omitted). *See also* State v. Jones, 84 Wash. 2d 823, 529 P.2d 1040 (1974) in which the Supreme Court of Washington stated that the words "know" and "appreciate" in the ALI test are not synonomous and are to be given their ordinary meanings.

42. United States v. Brawner, 471 F.2d 969, 1027 (D.C. Cir. 1972) (Bazelon, C.J., concurring in part and dissenting in part). *See id*. at 1025-28 for a more extensive discussion of Judge Bazelon's position.

43. *Id*. at 1028. *But cf*. McDonald v. United States, 312 F.2d 847 (D.C. Cir. 1962), in which the court attempted to use "mental disease" as a legal concept.

44. *Id*. at 1029 (footnote omitted).

45. MODEL PENAL CODE § 4.01, Comments, at 160 (Tent. Draft No. 4, 1955).

46. J. Biggs, THE GUILTY MIND 160 (Baltimore: Johns Hopkins Press, 1955).

47. Diamond, *From M'Naghten to Currens, and Beyond*, 50 CALIF. L. REV. 189, 194 (1962).

48. Kuh, *A Prosecutor Considers the Model Penal Code*, 63 COLUM. L. REV. 608, 626 (1963).

49. Royal Commission on Capital Punishment, *supra* note 5, at 116.

50. The proposal appears as alternative (a) to paragraph (1) of Model Penal Code § 4.01:

A person is not responsible for criminal conduct if at the time of such conduct as a result of mental disease or defect his capacity either to appreciate the criminality of his conduct or to conform his conduct to the requirements of law is so substantially impaired that he cannot justly be held responsible. MODEL PENAL CODE § 4.01, (Tent. Draft No. 4, 1955) (footnote omitted).

In Wechsler, *supra* note 15, at 372, Professor Wechsler explains why the language of his proposed test is preferable to that of the Royal Commission.

51. United States v. Brawner, 471 F.2d 969, 1032 (D.C. Cir. 1972) (Bazelon, C.J., concurring in part and dissenting in part) (emphasis omitted).

52. *Id.* at 1010-11 (footnote omitted).

53. *Id.* at 1019 (footnote omitted).

54. *Id.* at 1032 (footnote omitted).

55. Royal Commission on Capital Punishment, *supra* note 5, at 286-87.

56. United States v. Brawner, 471 F.2d 969, 989 (D.C. Cir. 1972).

57. Washington v. United States, 390 F.2d 444, 462 (D.C. Cir. 1967) (Fahy, J., concurring specially in affirmance).

58. Note, *Criminal Law–Guidelines for Expert Testimony in the Insanity Defense–Making the "Product" Palpable*, 18 DePAUL L. REV. 812, 819-20 (1969).

59. A. Goldstein, *supra* note 7, at 81-82.

60. American Bar Foundation, *supra* note 6, at 385.

61. *Id.*

62. A. Goldstein, *supra* note 7, at 53-54 (footnote omitted).

63. A. Matthews, MENTAL DISABILITY AND THE CRIMINAL LAW 44 (Chicago: American Bar Foundation, 1970).

64. *See* cases cited in A. Goldstein, *supra* note 7, at 238 n.27.

65. State v. Griffin, 99 Ariz. 43, 48-49, 406 P.2d 397, 400 (1965) (citations omitted).

66. *Id.* at 48-49, 406 P.2d at 401.

67. A. Goldstein, *supra* note 7, at 56.

68. *Id.* at 59-60.

69. *Id.* at 64.

70. State v. Carlson, 5 Wis. 2d 595, 93 N.W.2d 354 (1958).

71. State v. Wolak, 26 N.J. 464, 140 A.2d 385 (1958). *See also* State v. Griffin, 99 Ariz. 43, 406 P.2d 397 (1965), where the supreme court reversed the trial court's exclusion of psychiatric testimony on the defendant's background and on his mental defects or abnormalities upon which the psychiatrist based his ultimate opinion.

72. A. Goldstein, *supra* note 7, at 78-79.

73. United States v. Brawner, 471 F.2d 969, 1015 n.13 (D.C. Cir. 1972) (Bazelon, C.J., concurring in part and dissenting in part).

74. American Bar Foundation, *supra* note 6, at 385-86.

75. S. Glueck, LAW AND PSYCHIATRY: COLD WAR OR *ENTENTE CORDIALE* 116 n.52 (Baltimore: Johns Hopkins Press, 1966) *quoting* H.R. Rep. No. 563, 87th Cong., 1st Sess. (1961) *commenting on* H.R. 7052.

76. R. Simon, THE JURY AND THE DEFENSE OF INSANITY 203 (Boston: Little, Brown and Co., 1967).

77. *Id*. at 204.

78. President's Commission on Crime in the District of Columbia, REPORT 550 (Washington, D.C.: Government Printing Office, 1966).

79. United States v. Brawner, 471 F.2d 969, 989 (D.C. Cir. 1972).

80. A. Matthews, *supra* note 63, at 63-64.

81. R. Simon, *supra* note 76.

82. *Id*. at 192.

83. *Id*. at 216. *But cf*. American Bar Foundation, *supra* note 6, at 386, where this conclusion is disputed.

84. R. Simon, *supra* note 76, at 200.

85. James, *Status and Competence of Jurors*, 65 AM. J. SOC. 563, 565 (1959).

86. Arens, Granfield, and Susman, *Jurors, Jury Charges and Insanity*, 14 CATH. U.L. REV. 1, 11 (1965).

87. *Id*. at 22.

88. *Id*. at 13.

89. Comment, *The Psychiatrist's Role in Determining Accountability for Crimes: The Public Anxiety and an Increasing Expertise*, 52 MARQ. L. REV. 380, 390 (1969) (footnotes omitted).

90. *Id*. at 394.

91. United States v. Brawner, 471 F.2d 969, 1030 (D.C. Cir. 1972) (Bazelon, C.J., concurring in part and dissenting in part).

92. A. Goldstein, *supra* note 7, at 63.

93. Diamond, *From Durham to Brawner, a Futile Journey*, 1973 WASH. U.L.Q. 109.

94. *Id*. at 115.

95. United States v. Brawner, 471 F.2d 969, 1039 (D.C. Cir. 1972) (Bazelon, C.J., concurring in part and dissenting in part).

96. American Bar Foundation, *supra* note 6, at 392.

97. Chief Justice Joseph Weintraub has asserted his unwillingness to depart from the *M'Naghten* test, "until a basis for personal blameworthiness can be scientifically demonstrated . . . ." State v. Lucas, 30 N.J. 37, 83, 152 A.2d 50, 75 (1959) (Weintraub, C.J., concurring).

98. A. Goldstein, *supra* note 7, at 66.

99. Beltran v. United States, 302 F.2d 48, 52-53 (1st Cir. 1962).

100. *See, e.g.,* People v. Kelly, 10 Cal. 3d 565, 578-82, 516 P.2d 875, 884-87, 111 Cal. Rptr. 171, 180-83 (1973) (Mosk, J., concurring).

101. 471 F.2d 969 (D.C. Cir. 1972).

102. For a discussion of the various positions taken by amici, *see* Allen, *The Brawner Rule–New Lyrics for an Old Tune*, 1973 WASH. U.L.Q. 67, 70-73.

103. The majority opinion, written by Judge Leventhal for eight members of the court, is forty-one pages long. Chief Judge Bazelon wrote a separate twenty-nine page opinion in which he concurred in the result that the *Durham* rule be abandoned but advocated adoption of the justly responsible test instead of the ALI test.

104. United States v. Brawner, 471 F.2d 969, 979 (D.C. Cir. 1972).

105. A. Goldstein, *supra* note 7, at 93.

106. *Id.* at 95.

107. The recommended language is similar to the language in the proposed Michigan Revised Criminal Code. MICH. REV. CRIM. CODE § 705 (Final Draft, 1967).

108. *See* discussion in text pp. 15 and 17-18 *supra*.

109. United States v. Eichberg, 439 F.2d 620, 626-27 (D.C. Cir. 1971) (Bazelon, C.J., concurring) (footnotes omitted).

110. Pugh, *The Insanity Defense in Operation: A Practicing Psychiatrist Views Durham and Brawner*, 1973 WASH. U.L.Q. 87, 103-104 (footnotes omitted).

111. *See* discussion in text p. 15 *supra*, for the *McDonald* definition.

112. United States v. Brawner, 471 F.2d 969, 984 (D.C. Cir. 1972).

113. *Id.* at 1011 (Bazelon, C.J., concurring in part and dissenting in part).

114. Pugh, *supra* note 110, at 104-105 (footnotes omitted).

115. *See* United States v. Eichberg, 439 F.2d 620, 626 (D.C. Cir. 1971) (Bazelon, C.J., concurring).

116. 290 F.2d 751 (3d Cir. 1961).

117. *Id.* at 774 n.32.

118. Comment, *The Insanity Defense Under the Michigan Revised Criminal Code*, 14 WAYNE L. REV. 863, 876-77 (1968).

119. *See, e.g.,* United States v. Brawner, 471 F.2d 969 (D.C. Cir. 1972); Wade v. United States, 426 F.2d 64 (9th Cir. 1970); United States v.

Freeman, 357 F.2d 606 (2d Cir. 1966); Wion v. United States, 325 F.2d 420 (10th Cir. 1963).

120. United States v. Brawner, 471 F.2d 969, 992 (D.C. Cir. 1972).

121. *Id.*

122. Weihofen, *Capacity to Appreciate "Wrongfulness" or "Criminality" Under the A.L.I.-Model Penal Code Test of Mental Responsibility*, 58 J. CRIM. L.C. & P.S. 27 (1967).

123. *See* discussion in text p. 18 *supra*.

124. Wade v. United States, 426 F.2d 64 (9th Cir. 1970).

125. *Id.* at 73.

3 Procedural Issues in Insanity Determinations

Overview: Procedural Disabilities of the Defendant

Apparently a popular belief exists that the insanity ". . . defense is a great benefit to the defendant, who can readily purchase psychiatric testimony and thus have an easy way out of criminal liability."[1] If there really is such a benefit, why is the defense raised so infrequently? Writers have supplied two answers: (1) "the specter of indeterminate detention"[2] if the defendant successfully pleads the defense (an issue to be discussed in the next portion of this book[3] and (2) procedural disadvantages to the defendant who relies on the insanity plea (an issue discussed in this portion of the book).

In reality, the overwhelming number of criminal defendants, including those mentally disordered, are indigent. A study prepared for the American Bar Foundation[4] reports on the adverse affects of indigence on a defendant's chances of preparing and successfully presenting an insanity defense even if the defendant is willing to accept the prospect of indeterminate hospitalization. First, an indigent defendant is usually unable to make bond and thus remains in jail pending trial. The prosecution has available to it testimony of those observing his behavior during this pre-trial detention and also can obtain notice of any visits by a psychiatrist who examines the defendant. In essence, the prosecution has early knowledge that the defendant's counsel is considering an insanity defense.[5]

Second, conditions in the jail create problems for the defendant in dealing with psychiatrists. He may have difficulties in persuading a psychiatrist to examine him in jail because of the inadequate clinical facilities there. Thus, the indigent defendant may be unable to secure the services of a psychiatrist whose testimony might be favorable to his case. Moreover, in the inherently coercive atmosphere, an imprisoned defendant may be unable to resist an examination by prosecution psychiatrists or by supposedly impartial experts.[6]

Third, the indigent defendant may not be able to obtain necessary psychiatric treatment while he remains in the county jail. Jails do not have psychiatric personnel to treat inmates, and private psychiatrists are usually unwilling to conduct therapy there. Aside from benefits of the therapy itself, the indigent, imprisoned defendant is deprived of another benefit. The existence of a therapeutic relationship is often viewed as a positive factor for defendants in plea bargaining, in jury deliberations, and in sentencing considerations.[7]

Fourth, many states permit the trial court to appoint impartial experts to examine the defendant's mental condition after the insanity defense has been formally raised. Thus, the defendant is placed at a strategical disadvantage in raising the defense, for he must commit himself in advance to the opinion of these experts, whom he is not permitted to choose.[8]

Fifth, the study found that these presumably impartial experts in fact tend to favor the prosecution.[9] Such experts are usually associated with the public mental hospital system and tend to view mental illness from a different perspective than do doctors in private practice. Often the court-appointed expert equates insanity with psychosis, thereby requiring that the illness invade every aspect of the personality and completely immobilize it.[10]

Sixth, because the prosecution receives a copy of the expert's report and because that report is often favorable to the prosecution, the indigent defendant's plea bargaining power is weakened.[11]

Seventh, the defendant's plea bargaining power

> . . . is also undermined by the fact that making the insanity plea is tantamount to a virtual confession that the defendant did the acts charged. If the state's case is less than conclusive, as often it is, a chance for acquittal is sacrificed.[12]

Eighth, statutes calling for mental examinations by impartial experts often provide for lengthy inpatient hospitalization for psychiatric examination. However, the researchers discovered that such confinement does not generally produce a more in-depth evaluation. In fact, there is no assurance that more than a superficial examination has taken place, even though the inpatient confinement may last for thirty, sixty, or ninety days.

> At the staff conferences we observed in one institution, the actual psychiatric examination—the interval when patient-accused is face to face with doctor—lasted between five and twelve minutes.[13]

Ninth, defense lawyers are usually unwilling to make the investment of time required to present the complicated issues involved in the insanity defense. Frequently, defense counsel is a court-appointed attorney who desires to avoid a prolonged trial because he will receive no additional compensation for his extended labors. Moreover, most lawyers are familiar with the conventional criminal process and can make educated guesses concerning what will happen to their clients at various stages of the proceedings, including the maximum sentence likely to be imposed. The insanity defense, however, places most criminal lawyers on uncertain ground.[14]

Dean Goldstein has noted that at the present time the procedural scales are heavily weighted against the insanity defense and in favor of a guilty plea.[15] The recommendations contained in this portion of my book will seek to better balance these scales. In my opinion, a society that recognizes an insanity defense must assure to those it prosecutes the opportunity to present the best possible defense.

Raising the Defense

Traditionally, a defendant who is competent to stand trial is regarded as competent also to decide which defenses to plead and present. Nevertheless, there have been some court decisions—primarily in the District of Columbia[16]—holding that the prosecutor or the court may raise the insanity defense over the objection of the defendant and defense counsel. By successfully pleading the defense, a prosecutor might achieve a lengthier confinement of the defendant than might be achieved through criminal conviction. However, the United States Supreme Court case of *Lynch v. Overholser*[17] has placed this practice in doubt. In *Lynch,* the Court held that the defendant could not be confined pursuant to the District's mandatory commitment statute following acquittal by reason of insanity when he had elected not to raise the insanity defense but had had it forced upon him by the prosecution. Dean Goldstein states:

> *Lynch* will probably emerge as authority for the proposition that neither prosecutor nor judge can assert the insanity defense when a competent defendant, who is adequately represented, has chosen not to do so. There is no more reason for the prosecutor or judge to displace defense counsel with regard to the insanity defense than there is in the case of alibi or entrapment or a coerced confession or an unlawful search. All that can reasonably be asked is that the guilty plea be supervised sufficiently closely to assure that the abandonment of defenses takes place after adequate advice.[18]

In most states the defense of insanity is not pleaded separately; rather it is included under a general plea of "not guilty." A majority of states permit the defense to be pleaded at trial. However, due to the problems of proof inherent in a plea of insanity, approximately twenty states require that adequate notice be given to the prosecution before trial. Some require the insanity plea be entered at the time of arraignment; others specify that notice of intent to rely on the defense be given a designated number of days before trial.[19]

The notice requirements have been challenged unsuccessfully in a number of states as infringing upon defendant's privilege against self-incrimination.[20] Although the United States Supreme Court has not resolved the issue, it has held that a defendant may constitutionally be required to give prior notice of his intention to rely upon an alibi defense.[21] To the extent that the insanity defense involves an admission that the defendant committed the criminal act with which he is charged, the claim of privilege against self-incrimination may be more supportable for the insanity defense than it is for the alibi defense.

If a notice provision is desirable and constitutional, what is to be done with belated attempts to raise the defense? In answering this question, one should remember that: (1) as a practical matter reliance on the insanity defense is tantamount to an admission that the defendant committed the act charged; (2) an unsuccessful insanity defense increases significantly the chance of conviction; and (3) a successful insanity defense almost always results in indeterminate confinement. Because of these disadvantages, defense counsel may appropriately defer a decision to plead insanity until late in the preparation of his case. From a defense strategy, any other defense is preferable. A defendant who for any legitimate reason has failed to give timely notice should not be deprived of the defense. Strict adherence to the notice requirement is unduly harsh. Less drastic measures, including delay of the beginning of trial, can be employed to protect the prosecutor from the effects of a defendant's belated notice.

I propose the following statute:

Notice of intent to defend on the ground of irresponsibility shall be served on the prosecuting attorney a sufficient time before trial to enable the prosecution to prepare to meet the defense. On the motion of the prosecutor, the court may grant a delay or suspension of proceedings in a case when notice was not given a sufficient time before trial.

The Burden of Proof

The burden of proof issue consists of two subissues: (1) the initial burden of going forward with the evidence (the production burden) and (2) the ultimate burden of persuading the jury (the persuasion burden).

Because most people are sane, the law presumes that an individual defendant is sane. This presumption relieves the prosecution of having to establish the defendant's sanity in each criminal case. In all jurisdictions, the initial burden of presenting evidence of insanity is placed upon the defendant. However, the states are not in agreement as to the quantum of evidence required to discharge the production burden. Some require that the evidence be sufficient "to raise a reasonable doubt" of the defendant's mental responsibility for the criminal act; others merely require that "some" evidence, "slight" evidence, "any" evidence, or "evidence" be presented.

By presuming sanity absent the defendant's evidence to the contrary, "the law weights the scales against the insanity defense."[22] Theoretically, if a defendant fails to discharge the production burden, the trial court should preclude him from relying on the insanity defense. However, Dean Goldstein discovered that in practice little evidence is needed to satisfy the production burden. Lay testimony that the defendant "seemed abnormal" is sufficient. Because the insanity defense is usually raised only in cases of serious crime, judges are not inclined to take the case from the jury by ruling that the defendant did not meet the production burden.[23]

Once evidence of insanity has been introduced to adequately satisfy the production burden, the burden of persuasion is in issue. The federal government[24] and twenty-six states require the prosecution to establish the defendant's responsibility beyond a reasonable doubt. Twenty-five states require the defendant to establish his irresponsibility by a preponderance of the evidence (see Appendix A-2).

The decision on which party to place the burden of persuasion may be crucially significant because presenting conclusive evidence on the insanity issue is virtually impossible for either party. Those who would place the persuasion burden on the prosecution argue that the two basic elements of a crime are a criminal act (*actus reus*) and a criminal intent (*mens rea*). The issue of criminal responsibility focuses on the defendant's capacity to have the requisite criminal intent. Society presumes the innocence of the accused and imposes upon the prosecution the burden of proving the defendant's guilt beyond a reasonable doubt. Because guilt cannot be proven (in any case in which it is raised as an issue) without proof of the defendant's mental capacity to commit the crime, the prosecution must bear the burden of proof on this essential issue. If the burden of persuasion is placed on the accused, he would be forced to disprove an essential element of the crime, and this is no more appropriate than requiring him to disprove commission of a criminal act.

Those who would place the persuasion burden on the defendant perceive the issue of criminal irresponsibility as an affirmative defense to be proved by the defendant rather than as an element of the criminal charge to be proved by the prosecution. In their opinion, the presumption of innocence that usually justifies placing the burden of persuasion on the prosecution is offset by the presumption of sanity that justifies placing the burden of persuasion on the defendant when his sanity is in question. Adherents to this view are concerned that a defendant will always be able to satisfy the production burden by creating at least a doubt about his sanity. Thus, he may be able to escape criminal responsibility unless the burden of persuasion is also placed on him.[25]

In my opinion, those who favor placing the burden of persuasion on the defendant do not realistically evaluate the difficulties he encounters in attempting to prove the defense. According to the American Bar Foundation, the state has the means to obtain expensive psychiatric testimony that may be essential to the determination of criminal responsibility. As a practical matter, indigent defendants lack such resources.[26] Also, Judge Bazelon has asserted that the indigent defendant's limited access to expert psychiatric assistance requires placement of the persuasion burden on the prosecution.[27]

In *Davis v. United States,*[28] the United States Supreme Court held that in federal cases, the burden of persuasion is on the prosecution to prove the defendant sane beyond a reasonable doubt. However, in *Leland v. Oregon,*[29] the Supreme Court upheld the constitutionality of a state statute, since repealed, that placed the burden of proving insanity on the defendant. Although *Leland* clearly holds that due process does not guarantee any particular allocation of the persuasion burden, that holding appears to have been severely undercut by the recent Supreme Court decision of *In re Winship.*[30]

In *Winship,* the Court held that the reasonable doubt standard of proof is required in state juvenile delinquency hearings. Justice Brennan, writing for the Court, extended the proof requirement beyond the juvenile delinquency context, stating:

> Lest there remain any doubt about the constitutional stature of the reasonable-doubt standard, we explicitly hold that the Due Process Clause protects the accused against conviction except upon proof beyond a reasonable doubt of every fact necessary to constitute the crime with which he is charged.[31]

In evaluating the significance of *Winship,* one author noted:

> Since a defendant's sanity, once put in issue, is clearly a necessary element for a criminal conviction, *Winship* strongly suggests that due process requires sanity, like any other necessary element, to be shown by the prosecution beyond a reasonable doubt. This conclusion is bolstered by the *Winship* Court's extensive reference, in quotations from *Davis* and Justice Frankfurter's *Leland* dissent, to the need for the reasonable doubt standard in conjunction with the insanity defense.[32]

I recommend that the legislature codify placement of a light (any evidence) burden of production on defendant and a heavy (beyond a reasonable doubt) burden of persuasion on the prosecution, by enacting the following statute:

> *In a criminal case in which the defendant has presented any evidence of irresponsibility, the burden of establishing beyond a reasonable doubt that the defendant was criminally responsible shall be on the prosecution.*

The Bifurcated Trial Concept

In 1927, the California Commission for the Reform of Criminal Procedure recommended creation of a separate plea of "not guilty by reason of insanity." If a defendant pleads "not guilty" and "not guilty by reason of insanity," a trial is held first on the "not guilty" plea alone. In this first trial, the defendant is conclusively presumed sane at the time the crime was committed. If the defendant is found guilty, a separate trial is held on the insanity plea. The defendant is criminally sentenced only if he is found criminally responsible in this second trial. California enacted legislation based on these recommendations, and the legislation is still in effect.[33]

Professors David W. Louisell and Geoffrey C. Hazard, Jr., who examined in detail California's bifurcated trial concept,[34] state that the California Commission was "prosecution-minded" and ". . . seems to have regarded the claim of insanity as a sham defense used by the obviously guilty to gull juries into verdicts of acquittal."[35] In the words of the Commission, the purpose of establishing a bifurcated trial procedure was to eliminate the defendant's ability

> . . . to submit to the jury great masses of evidence having no bearing upon the question of whether the offense was committed. This is frequently made the basis for appeals to the sympathy or prejudice of the jury and even though this is not done, often introduces great confusion into the trial.[36]

The American Bar Foundation charges that by separating the trials of guilt and sanity, the Commission assumed it was possible to separate criminal intent from sanity and to determine whether the defendant committed a criminal act without examining his intent. Both assumptions are suspect.[37]

The attempt to separate the issue of guilt from the issue of the defendant's mental condition has not succeeded in California. In *People v. Wells*,[38] the Supreme Court of California held that evidence concerning a defendant's mental condition is admissible in the guilt/innocence stage of the trial to show that he did not possess the specific intent required for the crime charged, even though his mental condition at the time of the criminal act does not meet the insanity test. Thus, the court accepted the doctrine of diminished responsibility and implied that refusal to admit evidence demonstrating lack of specific intent in the guilt/innocence stage of the trial would be a denial of due process.[39]

The *Wells* decision has been subjected to severe criticism. Professors Louisell and Hazard state that the court had to engage in "some rather strenuous legal gymnastics"[40] in order to rule that evidence tending to show that a certain mental condition *could* not exist—that is, the defendant was insane—is not admissible in the guilt/innocence stage of the trial but that evidence tending to show that a certain mental condition *did* not exist—that is, the specific intent required for the crime was not present—is admissible. "[O]f course, proof that something could not exist is the best possible evidence that it did not exist."[41] In his dissent in *Wells*, Justice Carter wrote:

> It is strange reasoning to say that you may prove a partial mental quirk or disability to refute the presence of intent but cannot give evidence of a total mental aberration. This is equivalent to saying that blindness in one eye will absolve a person from guilt, but that two sightless eyes will constitute no defense. Is this not a paradoxical absurdity?[42]

After reviewing the California bifurcation cases, Professors Louisell and Hazard conclude:

> The separate trial procedure, as it stands today, results in duplication. The proof admissible to show defendant's mental state at the time of the crime is substantially the same as that admissible to show insanity. No workable rule has been formulated, and probably none can be formulated, that would effectively differentiate between the two types of evidence.
>
> The separate trial procedure was based on an inadequate premise of law. It assumed that the issue of guilt and the issue of mental condition are separable. We submit that reason shows they are not separable, and that experience confirms this conclusion. We therefore believe that the separate trial procedure should be abolished.[43]

Two governor's commissions have recommended that the California bifurcation statute be repealed as no longer serving a useful purpose.[44]

Although some states experimented with the bifurcated trial concept, it remains statutorily intact and mandatory only in California and Colorado.[45] Even when bifurcation is ordered in Colorado, evidence of diminished responsibility—that is, did the defendant, due to his mental condition, lack the intent necessary for a specific intent crime—has been held to be admissible in the guilt/innocence stage of the trial.[46] Texas, Louisiana, and Arizona have recently abandoned bifurcation.

The bifurcated trial has been viewed as "a concept of the past."[47] Admission of evidence on the defendant's state of mind in the guilt/innocence trial results in repetition of similar evidence in the sanity/insanity trial. However, elimination of such evidence in the first trial denies the defendant his due process right to introduce all relevant evidence prior to the determination of guilt.[48]

Nevertheless, reasons remain for retaining some form of bifurcation. When a defendant wishes to present both a defense on the merits and an insanity defense, each issue may suffer from joint presentation in one trial. Introduction of evidence that the defendant was insane at the time he committed the criminal act presupposes that the act in question was committed. Such evidence may contaminate the guilt/innocence decision. Bifurcation avoids the necessity of the defendant asserting inconsistent theories in the same proceeding.

A bifurcated trial has been endorsed as:

> . . . a valuable procedural device for protecting defendants' fifth amendment rights when a compulsory psychological examination has been conducted on behalf of the prosecution. . . . In a single trial, if a psychological examiner to whom incriminating admissions have been made is placed on the witness stand, there is arguably a significant danger that he may unintentionally disclose those admissions. Even if he does not, it may be impossible to explain or attack his opinion without reference to such admissions. The result is that he is either permitted to testify regarding those admissions or his testimony is not fully explained or subjected to full attack. Moreover, there is a strong possibility that a jury may infer from the examiner's willingness to testify that he is satisfied as to the commission of the acts and that his satisfaction stems from what he learned during the examination.[49]

The proper issue is not whether bifurcation should be retained, but rather where bifurcation should occur in the trial. By dividing the trial into a guilt/innocence stage and a mental capacity stage, legislatures created a problem of constitutional dimensions. Because the defendant is presumed sane in the first stage, he is improperly denied the right to disprove a material element of the crime—that is, lack of mental capacity—*prior* to a determination of guilt. If, however, the case is divided into an *act* stage and a guilt/innocence stage, bifurcation poses no problem. Thus, if a defendant wants to assert that no criminal act has been committed or that he is not the individual who committed the criminal act, he would be able to do so and to have these issues determined before evidence on the insanity defense is admitted. Only if the jury finds adversely to the defendant in the first stage of the trial, would the insanity issue be introduced in the guilt/innocence stage to question the defendant's criminal responsibility. Because the psychiatrists often assume that the act was committed, their testimony should be excluded from the first stage. This exclusion avoids an unsupported finding by the jury that the defendant committed the act. If the jury concludes on the basis of other evidence presented in the first stage that the defendant committed the act, a full discussion of the defendant's mental capacity at the time he acted is appropriate.[50]

Bifurcation should be retained in a modified form that will result in neither duplication of evidence nor prejudice to the defendant's case.

I recommend that the legislature enact the following statute:

> *In a criminal case in which defendant has served notice of intent to defend on the ground of irresponsibility, the trial court shall order, upon defendant's request, that evidence shall be presented first on whether defendant committed the act that would constitute the crime if the requisite mental state for criminal responsibility is also proven. At the completion of the presentation of this evidence, the jury shall determine whether the act was committed by the defendant.*
>
> *If the jury finds that the act was not committed by the defendant, the court shall enter a judgment of not guilty. If the jury finds that the act was committed by the defendant, the trial shall resume before the same jury, which shall hear evidence on*

whether the requisite mental state for criminal responsibility existed at the time defendant acted. At the completion of the presentation of this evidence, the jury shall determine the guilt or innocence of the defendant.

This proposal permits evidence of the insanity defense to be admitted only in the second stage of the bifurcated procedure. The concept of diminished responsibility, discussed and endorsed in a subsequent portion of this book,[51] expands beyond the sanity/insanity inquiry the admissibility of evidence relating to a defendant's mental condition. With bifurcation, evidence of diminished responsibility would also be presented in the trial's second stage. Thus, where diminished responsibility is accepted, the words "*requisite mental state for criminal responsibility*" should be altered to clarify that evidence on whether the defendant possessed the necessary criminal intent is reserved for the second portion of the trial.

I realize that dividing the trial into an act stage and a guilt/innocence stage raises the question of whether issues other than mental capacity belong in the first or in the second stage. I prefer limiting the act stage to evidence showing whether the defendant was the human agency who set in motion the events that might be proven to be a crime and expanding the guilt/innocence stage to include all other considerations. I favor this approach to minimize the possibility of the jury misconstruing the first stage as a guilt/innocence stage. A complete resolution of these problems is beyond the scope of this book, but these problems should not deter legislative acceptance of bifurcation as recommended above.

The Expert: Assistance, Examination, and Testimony

The use of psychiatrists in the insanity defense poses three major questions: (1) Is an indigent defendant entitled to psychiatric assistance in preparing his defense? (2) Can a defendant be compelled to undergo a psychiatric examination prior to trial? (3) Are there appropriate limitations that should be placed on psychiatric testimony at trial?

Expert Assistance to the Defense

Dean Goldstein has asserted that in order for our criminal justice system to work, "the parties must be comparable in litigating resources. At a minimum, each must be represented by counsel and have investigative and expert aid to assure that the representation is effective."[52] Insofar as the insanity defense is concerned, courts have repeatedly held that expert testimony is not essential. However, a defendant relying solely on lay testimony will have difficulty in presenting a strong case.

In practical terms, a successful defense without expert testimony will be made only in cases so extreme, or so compelling in sympathy for the defendant, that the prosecutor is unlikely to bring them at all.[53]

Often courts construe an indigent defendant's request for psychiatric assistance as a request for an expert witness who will testify in his favor. Courts have not been disposed to provide such a witness.[54] They reason that in examining the defendant and in testifying, the psychiatrist must remain impartial and that the defendant cannot demand they find him a friendly expert. The courts' attitude is not affected by the ability of the affluent defendant to seek out and obtain favorable psychiatric testimony.

However, a psychiatrist's assistance is needed for purposes other than testifying at trial. Because the adversarial process requires that each side attempt to neutralize the evidence of the other, the defendant has a right to cross-examine all witnesses, including psychiatrists, whose opinions are damaging to his case. Judge Bazelon recognizes the legitimate need for psychiatric assistance to defense counsel to insure vigorous cross-examination:

[I]f an indigent patient needs and is entitled to a lawyer, far more may he also need the assistance of a psychiatrist in the preparation of his case. This court has often pointed out the difficulty a lawyer untutored in the arcane mysteries of psychiatry may encounter when appointed to represent an indigent who is mentally disturbed. If the attorney is cut off from all sources of expert assistance on these matters, the patient may be effectively denied his right to an adversarial determination of his [sanity] . . . .

An independent psychiatrist rendering such assistance must of course distinguish scrupulously between his role as an impartial expert in reporting to the court and testifying, and his role as an advisor on psychiatric matters for the patient's counsel. Delicate questions will, of course, arise. But an independent psychiatrist could, it would seem, advise an attorney of the nature of his indigent client's mental abnormalities, the degree of uncertainty surrounding diagnoses of this sort of illness, and the lines of inquiry which might best help his client.[55]

Although a few courts have recognized the defendant's right to expert assistance in preparing his defense,[56] the issue has not been resolved satisfactorily. A recommendation for the resolution of this issue will follow a discussion of the impartial expert examination statutes.

Impartial Expert Examinations: Issues and Alternatives

In a majority of states (see Appendix A-3), statutes provide for a psychiatric examination of defendant on the issue of competency to stand trial, or on insanity, or on both. The stated objective of these statutes is the avoidance of ". . . the spectacle of the law's attempt to determine the issue of mental condition upon conflicting and contradictory testimony of hired partisan experts . . . ."[57] The impartial psychiatric examination is a device to provide ". . . a means by which the jury can be given a scientifically sound and unbiased presentation of the medical facts bearing on the accused's mental condition . . . ."[58]

Some states rely on the existence of an impartial expert statute to justify denial of funds to the defendant for the assistance of a friendly psychiatrist. These states reason that the expert may conclude that the defendant was insane and thus offer testimony supportive of the insanity defense. However, even if the impartial expert reaches a conclusion favorable to the defendant, his statutorily delineated function is limited to testimony at trial. He is not empowered to provide the defendant with assistance in preparing his case. Thus, the impartial expert statutes do not meet the needs of the indigent defendant.

As mentioned previously,[59] in the typical case the impartial expert's opinion tends to favor the prosecution. Moreover, not only are his report and testimony usually adverse to the defendant, but his supposed impartiality also gives his opinion added credence in the minds of the judge and jury.[60] A psychiatrist who was on the staff of St. Elizabeths Hospital in the District of Columbia expressed the view that "the expert witness dictates the verdict. . . . [T]he opinion of the psychiatrist who examines the defendant is almost certain to become the verdict of the court."[61]

> In the overwhelming majority of cases the hospital's report to the court is the sole determinant of the outcome of the insanity defense. If the hospital reports that the patient was sane at the time of the alleged act, the defense almost always abandons the insanity plea. Since over seventy-five percent of felons examined are reported as having been sane, the majority of insanity defenses are thus resolved before the case even comes to trial. If the hospital reports that the defendant was insane, the prosecution ceases to contest the issue.[62]

Dean Goldstein has attacked this aura of infallibility that seems to accompany the opinion of an impartial expert:

> If this added credibility coincided with an added ability to present the "truth," it would be difficult to reject the method which produced it. The impartial expert does not, however, bring "truth" with him. . . .
>
> An impartial expert, and the added credibility he brings with him, could be justified only if there was a high degree of consensus among psychiatrists on the answers to questions likely to arise in the courtroom, on the qualifications of persons competent to present such answers and on the techniques to be used at the various stages of examination. No such consensus can be said to exist.[63]

The expert's credibility may also be suspect in those states whose impartial expert statutes permit the same psychiatrist to investigate in one examination the defendant's competency to stand trial (present insanity) and his mental condition at the time of the supposed offense (past insanity). Although conducting a single examination on both issues is more economical, an evaluation of criminal responsibility may prejudice an evaluation of competency to stand trial. Because the questions in each evaluation are clearly distinguishable, the examinations should, in my opinion, be separated. If compentency to stand trial is an issue, examination should be on that issue alone. Only if the court determines that the defendant is competent and if the defendant raises the insanity defense, should there be another examination to evaluate his mental condition at the time of the alleged criminal act.

Impartial expert examination statutes have also been criticized[64] as violating the defendant's constitutional privilege against self-incrimination. This problem arises because in examining the defendant, the psychiatrist elicits statements from him in order to analyze the defendant's personality. A defendant participating in a psychiatric examination can incriminate himself in four ways:

> First, his admissions and statements may implicate him in the crime charged. Second, his statements and admissions may implicate him in other different crimes. Third, the evidence of his mental condition may help the state build its *prima facie* case by establishing the *mens rea* element (whether or not the defendant attempts an insanity defense). Finally, if the defendant raises the insanity defense, the compulsory examination has forced him to provide the state with evidence which might well defeat it.[65]

A number of state appellate courts have held that a defendant's fifth amendment rights are applicable in the context of a compulsory mental examination and that his participation cannot be compelled.[66] The American Bar Foundation concludes:

> [T]he movement toward expanded and more "impartial" psychiatric intervention in the criminal process is in need of clearer practical and constitutional justification. Court appointment does not assure impartiality, and may well deprive judge and jury of validly diverging opinions. Furthermore, whatever benefits are thought to be derived from expanded and nonadversary psychiatric intervention in the criminal process should be weighed against the element of compulsion inherent in this approach and the attendant possibilities of detention and incrimination without due process.[67]

In addition to difficulties with self-incrimination, it is virtually impossible to eliminate the undue influence on the jury of the impartial expert's testimony. Thus, I do not believe an impartial expert examination statute is warranted.

Nevertheless, I do recognize the prosecutor's legitimate need for a psychiatric evaluation of the defendant once the defendant has raised the insanity defense. Substitution of an expert selected by the prosecutor for an impartial expert appointed by the court eliminates the problem of the added credibility that attaches to "impartiality." If the prosecution expert's examination is restricted to a determination of the defendant's mental condition, and if the defendant is immunized against all adverse uses of his statements made at the examination, the incrimination problem is solved.[68]

I recommend that the legislature adopt the following statute in an attempt to reach this solution:

A defendant in a criminal case who has served notice of intent to defend on the ground of irresponsibility may be examined by a psychiatrist [*or other expert*] *selected by the prosecutor. The examination shall be limited to an evaluation of defendant's mental or emotional processes and behavior controls at the time the alleged criminal act was committed.*

1. **General Immunity.** *No evidence of any kind obtained from an examination by the prosecution psychiatrist* [*or other expert*] *shall be admissible at any proceeding to determine guilt or innocence unless the defendant first presents evidence of irresponsibility.*

2. **Specific Immunity.** *If defendant presents any evidence of irresponsibility, the following provisions shall apply:*

(a) No statement of the defendant obtained during an examination by the prosecution psychiatrist [*or other expert*]*, or evidence resulting from the statement, concerning the events which form the basis of the charges against the defendant shall be admissible at the trial of guilt or innocence, or at any subsequent proceeding to determine guilt or innocence.*

(b) No statement of the defendant obtained during an examination by the prosecution psychiatrist [*or other expert*]*, or evidence resulting from the statement, concerning any other events or transactions, shall be admissible at any proceeding to determine the defendant's guilt or innocence of criminal charges based on such events or transactions.*

(c) If the defendant consents, he may waive the specific immunities granted by either section 2(a) or 2(b) or both.[69]

The unavailability of psychiatrists in some rural areas may make necessary the addition of the words "*or other expert*" in the proposal.

The recommended statute is only one facet of the solution to the problem of self-incrimination. Similar proposals have been criticized:

Their complexity demands a great deal of attention from lawyers to issues and procedures which will be encountered quite infrequently in their practice. Thus it is quite possible the complex immunities . . . will not function effectively at the practical level. Expert testimony, for example, might remain as conclusory as at present, since the expert is forbidden to relate the direct admissions of the defendant, which will often be the most significant data at his disposal. The ideal solution relative to the problems discussed perhaps requires some sort of bifurcation.[70]

My bifurcation proposal[71] reduces the complexity of my prosecution expert/immunity proposals by restricting psychiatric testimony to the guilt/innocence stage of the trial. Prior to the introduction of any psychiatric testimony, commission of the alleged criminal act has been established. Thus, the bifurcation proposal, coupled with the prosecution expert/immunity proposals, alleviates the self-incrimination problem.

Obviously, neither existing impartial expert examination statutes nor my proposed prosecution expert/immunity statute deals adequately with the difficulties an indigent defendant has in obtaining adequate psychiatric assistance for preparation and presentation of the insanity defense.[72] The state should recognize its obligation to assure an indigent defendant the right to assert an effective insanity defense. I recommend that the legislature adopt the following statute:

No defendant in a criminal case who has served notice of intent to defend on the ground of irresponsibility shall be deprived of effective psychiatric [*or other expert*] *assistance because of his indigence. Upon the request of an indigent defendant, the court shall authorize the appointment of a private psychiatrist* [*or other expert*] *selected by the defendant at a reasonable fee to be paid by the state. Such fee shall include compensation for all services rendered by the psychiatrist* [*or other expert*] *in assisting in the preparation of the defense and in testifying at trial.*

The words "*or other expert*" in the recommended statute should be read in conjunction with the prosecution expert/immunity proposals. To neutralize the potential adverse testimony of the prosecution expert, the defendant must have the assistance of an equally qualified expert. Thus, if the defendant will be subjected to an examination by a prosecution psychiatrist, he should be entitled to the assistance of a psychiatrist whom he himself has chosen.

Limitations on Psychiatric Testimony

The overwhelming significance of expert testimony has been referred to repeatedly in this book. In fact, the proposed statute recognizing a defendant's right to psychiatric assistance is based primarily on the effect of psychiatric testimony on the jury. Without such assistance a defendant is unable to counterbalance adverse psychiatric testimony and is thus unable to present an effective defense.

My recommended move from *M'Naghten* to the more liberal ALI test increases the danger of expert domination of the jury decision. To avoid the jury's abdication of its function and acquiescence in the experts' stated conclusions, some authorities have proposed precluding psychiatric testimony on the ultimate issue of criminal responsibility—that is, barring insanity test questions. Dean Goldstein explains the proposal as follows:

The essential vice of allowing the test questions is that they tend to supplant the factual detail upon which the decision on responsibility should ideally be based.

Too often, psychiatric testimony consists of little else, as the test questions convert the insanity issue into what seems to be a search for something the psychiatric witnesses can "see"—like speed or weather, some seeing it one way and some another. The issue is treated as little more than a matter of credibility: which of the witnesses is to be believed? Which of them had a better vantage point, sharper eyes, less bias, etc.? The jury is left with the impression that it must choose between the experts, because it is not told enough about the defendant's mental life to enable it to make an intelligent judgment about *him*, rather than about the psychiatric witnesses. . . .

If the test questions are barred, counsel and witness will have no alternative but to present the details of the psychiatric investigation, placing the emphasis on the defendant rather than upon the psychiatrist or the legal formula. At the same time, the psychiatrist will be spared the discomfiture he feels when he is asked to speak in judgmental terms and the trial will be relieved of the bickering about the meaning of the words of the insanity defense. Given the extent to which the test questions have served as an irritant in the past and given the probability that the answers add little to the jury's understanding of the defendant and the issues, it would probably be best not to put the test questions to witnesses.[73]

In *Washington v. United States*,[74] the United States Court of Appeals for the District of Columbia, in construing the *Durham* rule then in effect in the District, held that psychiatrists are prohibited from testifying on whether the alleged offense was the "product" of mental illness because that determination is a part of the ultimate issue to be decided by the jury. Although that court abandoned the *Durham* test in favor of ALI in its decision in *United States v. Brawner*,[75] the court adhered to its decision in *Washington* insofar as that case requires the jury to be informed of the expert's underlying reasons and approach and not merely to be confronted with his ultimate opinions.

I propose that the legislature adopt the following statute precluding expert witnesses from testifying on the test questions of the insanity defense:

In a case in which the defendant's criminal responsibility is in issue, expert witnesses shall be precluded from expressing any opinion on whether, at the time he acted, defendant's mental or emotional processes or behavior controls were such that the jury could find him criminally irresponsible. Reaching a conclusion on the issue of defendant's criminal responsibility is solely a jury function.

Informing the Jury of the Effect of an Insanity Acquittal

Traditionally, juries are not permitted to consider the consequences of their verdicts. The jury's function is to determine guilt or innocence by finding the facts; speculation on the fate of the defendant is irrelevant to this function. The judge, not the jury, decides the post-verdict consequences.

Many jurisdictions rely on this separation of judge and jury functions to refuse a defendant's request for a jury instruction explaining that the defendant will be examined for commitment or automatically confined in a mental hospital if the verdict is not guilty by reason of insanity (see Appendix A-4). Some courts exclude such an instruction as being unduly favorable to the defendant. For example, in *State v. Garrett*,[76] the court asserted that the requested instruction

> . . . would divert the jury from the real merits of the insanity issue by the introduction of this extraneous consideration, which actually is nothing less than an invitation for the jury to find the defendant mentally irresponsible *because* he would then be confined anyway.[77]

However, there are valid reasons for informing the jury of the consequences of an insanity verdict. First, failure to inform the jury may unduly prejudice their decision against a valid insanity defense. "[A] jury, influenced by the specter of violent lunatics turned loose in the community, may 'convict, despite strong evidence of insanity at the time of the crime.'"[78] Second, research has disclosed that informing the jury of the consequences of an insanity verdict does not increase the number of such verdicts. Apparently many uninstructed jurors assume that the defendant will be confined for mental treatment after an acquittal by reason of insanity.[79] Third, in those states where an insanity acquittal does not automatically result in the defendant's indeterminate confinement in a mental hospital,[80] a jury instruction that the defendant will be detained for an examination of his present mental condition and possible civil commitment is not particularly advantageous to the defendant. Because civil commitment is not a certainty, the jury is not apt to be swayed toward an unwarranted insanity acquittal.

In *Lyles v. United States*,[81] the United States Court of Appeals for the District of Columbia Circuit, sitting en banc, ruled that the jury has a right to know the meaning of the insanity verdict unless there is an affirmative request by the defendant that such an instruction be omitted. For its decision, the court relied on the jurors' common knowledge of the consequences of guilty and not guilty verdicts and on their lack of common knowledge of the consequences of an insanity verdict. Informing the jury about the effect of an insanity acquittal equalizes their understanding.

I recommend that the legislature follow the approach taken in the *Lyles* case and adopt the following statute:

> *In a case in which the defendant's criminal responsibility is in issue, the court shall instruct the jury on the consequences of a verdict of acquittal by reason of irresponsibility unless the defendant requests that such instruction not be given.*

Notes

1. A. Matthews, MENTAL DISABILITY AND THE CRIMINAL LAW 36 (Chicago: American Bar Foundation, 1970). *See also* Louisell and Hazard, *Insanity as a Defense: The Bifurcated Trial*, 49 CALIF. L. REV., 805, 807-808 (1961).

2. A. Goldstein, THE INSANITY DEFENSE 167 (New Haven: Yale University Press, 1967).

3. *See* discussion in text pp. 61-73 *infra*.

4. A. Matthews, *supra* note 1.

5. *Id.* at 37-38.

6. *Id.* at 38.

7. *Id.*

8. *Id.* (footnote omitted).

9. *Id.* at 39.

10. *Id.* at 41-42.

11. *Id.* at 39.

12. *Id.* at 39 (footnote omitted).

13. *Id.* at 43.

14. *Id.* at 40.

15. A. Goldstein, *supra* note 2, at 186.

16. *See, e.g.,* Tatum v. United States, 190 F.2d 612 (D.C. Cir. 1951).

17. 369 U.S. 705 (1962). *See also* United States v. Wright, 511 F.2d 1311 (D.C. Cir. 1975) where the court held that the District's automatic commitment statute can not be applied to an insanity acquittee when the trial court raises the insanity defense *sua sponte*.

18. A. Goldstein, *supra* note 2, at 188.

19. *See* discussion in American Bar Foundation, THE MENTALLY DISABLED AND THE LAW 396 and table at 430-43, rev. ed., Brakel and Rock, eds. (Chicago: University of Chicago Press, 1971).

20. *See, e.g.,* State *ex rel.* Sikora v. District Court, 154 Mont. 241, 462 P.2d 897 (1969) and cases cited therein.

21. Williams v. Florida, 399 U.S. 78 (1970).

22. A. Goldstein, *supra* note 2, at 120.

23. *Id.* at 113.

24. *See* discussion in text of Davis v. United States, 160 U.S. 469 (1895), p. 44 *infra*.

25. *See, e.g.,* Ortwein v. Commonwealth, 76 Pa. 414, 425 (1874).

26. American Bar Foundation, *supra* note 19, at 400.

27. United States v. Brawner, 471 F.2d 969, 1036 (D.C. Cir. 1972) (Bazelon, C.J., concurring in part and dissenting in part).

28. 160 U.S. 469 (1895).

29. 343 U.S. 790 (1952).

30. 397 U.S. 358 (1970).

31. *Id.* at 364.

32. Comment, *Commitment of Persons Acquitted by Reason of Insanity: The Example of the District of Columbia*, 74 COLUM. L. REV. 733, 744 (1974) (footnote omitted).

33. CAL. PENAL CODE § 1026 (West 1970).

34. *See generally* Louisell and Hazard, *Insanity as a Defense: The Bifurcated Trial*, 49 CALIF. L. REV. 805 (1961).

35. *Id.* at 807, 808.

36. California Commission for the Reform of Criminal Procedure, REPORT 17 (1927).

37. American Bar Foundation, *supra* note 19, at 399 (footnote omitted). *See also* Comment, *The Gradual Decay of the Bifurcated Trial System in California and the Emergence of "Partial Insanity": 1966*, 3 CAL. WESTERN L. REV. 149, 150 (1967).

38. 33 Cal. 2d 330, 202 P.2d 53, *cert. denied*, 338 U.S. 836 (1949).

39. *Id.* at 351, 355, 202 P.2d at 66, 68.

40. Louisell and Hazard, *supra* note 34, at 818.

41. *Id.* at 819.

42. People v. Wells, 33 Cal. 2d 330, 360, 202 P.2d 53, 72 (Carter, J., dissenting), *cert. denied*, 338 U.S. 836 (1949).

43. Louisell and Hazard, *supra* note 34 at 829-30 (footnotes omitted).

44. Governor's Special Commissions on Insanity and Criminal Offenders, FIRST REPORT 30 (1962); Governor's Special Crime Study Commission, REPORT ON CRIMINAL LAW AND PROCEDURE 117 (1949).

45. COLO. REV. STAT. § 16-8-104 (1973).

46. COLO. REV. STAT. § 16-8-103(1) (1973); Becksted v. People, 133 Colo. 72, 292 P.2d 189 (1956).

47. American Bar Foundation, *supra* note 19, at 398.

48. *See* Dix, *Mental Illness, Criminal Intent, and the Bifurcated Trial*, 1970 LAW & THE SOCIAL ORDER (now Ariz. St. L.J.) 559, *discussing* State v. Shaw, 106 Ariz. 103, 471 P.2d 715 (1970).

49. *Id.* at 573-74 (footnotes omitted).

50. *Id.* at 574-75. *See also* Comment, *Due Process and Bifurcated Trials: A Double-Edged Sword*, 66 Nw. U.L. REV. 327, 341 (1971), where

the author suggests that if the entire ". . . case is tried before a single jury, bifurcation affects only the ordering, not the substance, of the issues. No defense is omitted; no evidence excluded."

51. *See* discussion in text pp. 75-83 *infra*.

52. A. Goldstein, *supra* note 2, at 123.

53. *Id*. at 124-25.

54. *See, e.g.*, Proctor v. Harris, 413 F.2d 383 (D.C. Cir. 1969); State v. Swanson, 9 Md. App. 594, 267 A.2d 270 (1970).

55. Proctor v. Harris, 413 F.2d 383, 389-90 (D.C. Cir. 1969) (Bazelon, C.J., concurring). The case from which this quotation was taken involved a habeas corpus petition seeking release from the mental hospital in which petitioner was confined following a verdict of not guilty by reason of insanity. Judge Bazelon's comment relates to the need for psychiatric assistance in such a proceeding. However, his comment is equally applicable to the criminal trial and the need for psychiatric assistance in the determination of criminal responsibility.

56. *See* People v. Watson, 36 Ill. 2d 228, 221 N.E.2d 645 (1966); State v. Hancock, 164 N.W.2d 330 (Iowa 1969).

57. Weihofen, *Procedure for Determining Defendant's Mental Condition Under the American Law Institute's Model Penal Code*, 29 TEMPLE L.Q. 235, 238 (1956).

58. *Id*.

59. *See* discussion in text p. 40 *supra*.

60. A. Goldstein, *supra* note 2, at 132.

61. Pugh, *The Insanity Defense in Operation: A Practicing Psychiatrist Views Durham and Brawner*, 1973 WASH. U.L.Q. 87, 91.

62. *Id*. at 89.

63. A. Goldstein, *supra* note 2, at 133.

64. *See, e.g.*, Danforth, *Death Knell for Pre-Trial Mental Examinations? Privilege Against Self-Incrimination*, 19 RUTGERS L. REV. 489 (1965); Lefelt, *Pretrial Mental Examinations: Compelled Cooperation and the Fifth Amendment*, 10 AM. CRIM. L. REV. 431 (1972); Note, *Requiring a Criminal Defendant to Submit to a Government Psychiatric Examination: An Invasion of the Privilege Against Self-Incrimination*, 83 HARV. L. REV. 648 (1970); Comment, *Changing Standards for Compulsory Mental Examinations*, 1969 WIS. L. REV. 270.

65. ARIZ. REV. STAT. ANN. 1973 Rules Crim. Proc. RULE 11.7 Comment.

66. *See* French v. District Court, 153 Colo. 10, 384 P.2d 268 (1963);

People v. Wax, 75 Ill. App. 2d 163, 220 N.E.2d 600 (1966); State v. Olson, 274 Minn. 225, 143 N.W.2d 69 (1966).

67. American Bar Foundation, *supra* note 19, at 403.

68. *See* Berry, *Self-incrimination and the Compulsory Mental Examination: A Proposal*, 15 ARIZ. L. REV. 919, 944 (1973). Copyright © 1973 by the Arizona Board of Regents. Reprinted by permission. Even if the impartial expert statutes are not replaced by prosecution expert statutes, the self-incrimination problem is eliminated by this approach.

69. This statute is derived from Rule 11.7, 1973 Arizona Rules of Criminal Procedure. ARIZ. REV. STAT. ANN. 1973 Rules Crim. Proc. RULE 11.7.

70. Berry, *supra* note 68, at 949.

71. *See* discussion in text pp. 47-48 *supra*.

72. Judge Bazelon has catalogued these difficulties in United States v. Brawner, 471 F.2d 969, 1036-38 (D.C. Cir. 1972) (Bazelon, C.J., concurring in part and dissenting in part).

73. A. Goldstein, *supra* note 2, at 103-104.

74. 390 F.2d 444 (D.C. Cir. 1967).

75. 471 F.2d 969 (D.C. Cir. 1972).

76. 391 S.W.2d 235 (Mo. 1965).

77. *Id*. at 242.

78. Tatum v. United States, 249 F.2d 129, 133 (D.C. Cir. 1948) (Bazelon, C.J., dissenting).

79. R. Simon, THE JURY AND THE DEFENSE OF INSANITY 92-93 (Boston: Little, Brown and Co., 1967).

80. *See* discussion in text pp. 61-73 *infra*.

81. 254 F.2d 725 (D.C. Cir. 1957).

4 Disposition of Persons Acquitted by Reason of Insanity

The Problems

Generally, an acquittal by reason of insanity does not result in freeing the defendant. As indicated in Appendix A-5, commitment to a mental institution[1] is automatic in seventeen states and is achievable in most others under a variety of procedures and standards. The appropriateness of mandatory commitment, however achieved, is a significant problem.

Mandatory post-acquittal commitment assumes that the criminal trial proved that the defendant should be institutionalized. This assumption would be warranted only if the trial had established that the defendant committed the criminal act, that he was insane at the time of the act, and that he continues to be insane. However, the trial does not establish these facts. Generally, there is no express finding by the jury that the defendant would have been found guilty of the crime had he not been found insane. Moreover, half the states place the ultimate burden of proof on the prosecution, and an insanity acquittal in those jurisdictions establishes only that the jury had a reasonable doubt about whether the defendant was sane. Even if a jurisdiction required that the jury determine specifically that the defendant committed the criminal act and that he had been insane at the time the act was committed, an indiscriminately applied presumption that the defendant's insanity continues at the time of disposition is not logical. The defendant who stood trial was assumed to be or was found to be competent to stand trial. The fact the trial was held at all undermines a presumption of continued insanity.[2]

A related problem is release from confinement.[3] Some states view insanity-acquittal commitment as therapeutic in purpose and focus on the individual's mental condition. They require that he be "restored to sanity," or "cured," or "no longer mentally ill," or "entirely and permanently recovered" in order to be eligible for release. Other states view the commitment as a form of preventive detention and focus on the dangerousness of the individual. They require that he no longer be dangerous in order to be eligible for release. Thus, a patient who is not mentally ill is denied release if he is still dangerous. Some states, focusing on both the mental condition and the dangerousness of the individual, require a restoration to sanity *and* a lack of dangerousness for eligibility for release. Strangely, some states permit release either if the patient is sane *or* if he is not dangerous. In these states a dangerous person will be released if he is sane; an insane person will be released if he is not dangerous.

The sanity criterion and the dangerousness criterion, as they are utilized in release statutes, have been criticized for their ambiguity.[4] For example, does a statute requiring that the patient be "restored to sanity" mean that he must be cured of mental illness completely or only that his mental condition be improved to the extent that it no longer meets the insanity test utilized by the state in its insanity defense? Does a statute requiring that the individual be "no longer dangerous" mean that there must be no recurrence of the same criminal act, or any criminal act, or any threatening conduct, or even something less? Must the lack of dangerousness, however defined, be established as an absolute certainty, or as a likelihood, or as a possibility, or even something less?

Perhaps the most significant problem involves the conditions of confinement. In most jurisdictions, the insanity-acquittee is confined in a special maximum security ward or institution where all "criminally insane" or "forensic" patients are housed.[5] Studies in various states support the conclusion that treatment in these facilities is virtually nonexistent and that "patients" are merely warehoused. For example, a United States district court made the following judgment of Farview State Hospital, Pennsylvania's maximum security hospital for the criminally insane:

> We cannot avoid the conclusion that medical-psychiatric treatment of inmates at Farview was grossly inadequate . . . . It is conceded that only three percent of the inhabitants of Farview received any therapeutic-psychiatric treatment.[6]

Inadequate treatment of "criminal order" patients confined in maximum security facilities is also demonstrated by comparing their release potential with that of other mental patients who are confined in non-maximum security facilities. The median stay of patients in Matteawan State Hospital, New York's maximum security facility for criminal order patients, is a minimum of *six to seven years*. The average length of hospitalization in other New York state hospitals is *four months*.[7]

The Final Report of the Ionia State Hospital Medical Audit Committee describes a patient's life inside Michigan's maximum security mental institution:

> The absolutely apathetic, empty existence that these men lead on the wards and the groping efforts which they follow to busy themselves with nothing, is terrible to behold. There was obviously little about which to be hopeful.
>
> The over concern for security is evident everywhere, and this reflects the poor understanding of the mission of the hospital, the culture which surrounds the hospital, and the lack of training for the security attendant staff. As one passes from building to building, one begins to feel somewhat like a mole. Obviously, it is not necessary to pass through the miles of tunnels in order to go from one building to

another. It is impossible to believe that this is the best way to provide security. The psychological oppressiveness of this system, in itself, makes it worthy of modification.[8]

A recent study of the Arizona State Hospital found that ". . . the true daily existence for the bulk of the patients is one of idleness and inactivity, occasionally sprinkled with staff and other patient contact."[9] Though the situation is described as "relatively bleak" for almost all patients, the report states that forensic patients, who are housed on the maximum security ward, experience the worst conditions. The 1969-70 Annual Report of the Arizona State Hospital describes their plight:

Maximum Security . . . continued to labor with the realities of obsolete crowded buildings, lack of proper treatment facilities, critical staff shortages, and the pressure of time. Idealistic program planning had to be put second to the demands for processing; mere management took precedence over treatment. . . .

[O]verall, conditions must be reported as discouraging. Staff turnover has been high in the face of frustrating obstacles. Recreation for patients is limited, industrial therapy is not available, and an educational effort proved abortive due to improper facilities. Court testimony consumes psychiatrists' time away from the unit. Under these conditions the primary medical treatment is chemotherapy. Appropriate rehabilitation, counseling, and education cannot even be attempted.[10]

Insanity acquittees who have been civilly committed to the Arizona State Hospital, as well as all patients confined on the maximum security unit, are on special classification. Requests for privileges for special classification patients must be approved by their residence unit, by the Special Classification Committee (hereinafter SCC), and by the hospital superintendent. The Arizona State Hospital study reports:

Some hospital staff members interviewed by the project expressed disappointment over what they termed the SCC's conservatism in granting privileges. Even in the face of a strong recommendation by those in closest contact with the patient, the privilege may be denied by the seven members of the SCC who probably know little about the patient and his therapeutic circumstances. Staff members indicated that the supposed SCC timidity is most apparent when the request involves patient contact with the community at large, such as with respect to off-grounds passes or contemplated discharges.[11]

The security orientation of hospital administrators who deal with patients acquitted by reason of insanity is attested to in a report prepared for the California Department of Mental Hygiene by Professor Herbert L. Packer.[12] His study on Atascadero State Hospital, California's maximum security mental institution, uncovered these deficiencies:

The Department has explicit statutory authorization to transfer patients in this category from one facility to another. It is questionable whether the flexibility afforded by the law is being adequately taken advantage of. There do not appear to be any criteria developed to determine fitness for transfer. An administrative review mechanism should be developed to insure continuous screening of this group to permit transfer at the earliest possible moment. . . .

A related problem is the tendency to take the seriousness of the criminal offense into account in determining the length of the patient's stay. Members of the staff readily admit this tendency in informal conversation. An extreme example is the unwritten "10-year rule," whereby patients who were charged with murder are not considered for release for that length of time. Granting the existence of public relations problems for the Hospital, the fact remains that it is a hospital not a prison and that patients are there for treatment rather than punishment. It is well known that murderers as a group have a low rate of recidivism and also that many assaultive psychotics who happen not to have killed as yet are more dangerous than some murderers. It should be Hospital policy to judge each PC 1026 [not guilty by reason of insanity] case on its facts without giving more weight to the nature of the offense charged than is relevant to a decision as to likelihood of recovery from mental illness.[13]

S.W. Morgan, M.D., the Superintendent and Medical Director of Atascadero, responded to the criticism of the Packer Report,[14] and according to Professor Packer, Dr. Morgan's "comments explicitly reject almost all of the recommendations for change made in the [Packer Report]."[15] The superintendent's attitude toward the "unwritten 10-year rule" criticism illustrates the continuing security orientation of his facility. In addition to admitting that patients acquitted of murder are not considered for *release* for ten years, Dr. Morgan revealed that they are not considered even for *transfer* out of Atascadero to a less secure facility for ten years.[16]

The tendency to consider the seriousness of the crime in determining length of stay at Atascadero is evidenced by a policy that allows patients acquitted of assault to be considered for release only after three years confinement.[17]

Dr. Morgan expressed his unwillingness to accept Professor Packer's suggestion that Atascadero should consider the nature of the offense charged only to the extent it is relevant in deciding the likelihood of recovery from mental illness. Dr. Morgan stated:

The present superintendent could not assume the responsibility and would need some kind of backup authority from the Director of DMH [Department of Mental Hygiene] to approve the release of 1026 P.C. [not guilty by reason of insanity] cases when dangerousness of the offense was not given top priority.[18]

Progress in Resolving the Problems

Recently courts have begun to examine mandatory commitment statutes, release criteria, and conditions of confinement; and some improvement in the law can be discerned. In *Bolton v. Harris,*[19] the Court of Appeals for the

District of Columbia, in construing the District's mandatory commitment statute, recognized the limitations of a verdict of not guilty by reason of insanity. In the opinion, Chief Judge Bazelon relied on the United States Supreme Court case of *Baxstrom v. Herold*[20] for the principle that ". . .the commission of criminal acts does not give rise to a presumption of dangerousness which, standing alone, justifies substantial difference in commitment procedures and confinement conditions for the mentally ill."[21] Thus, to commit to a mental hospital a person found not guilty of a crime by reason of insanity without affording him the procedural safeguards established under the civil commitment scheme constituted a denial of equal protection of the laws. The court rejected the argument, which had also been rejected by the Supreme Court in *Baxstrom,* that expeditious commitment of various categories of non-convict mentally ill persons is somehow justified because of the dangerous or criminal propensities of the individuals involved.

In *Specht v. Patterson,*[22] the United States Supreme Court held that a person convicted of taking indecent liberties[23] (maximum sentence of ten years) could not be sentenced under the Colorado Sex Offenders Act[24] (sentence of one day to life) without a full hearing. The imposition of the indeterminate sentence required a new finding of fact that was not an ingredient of the offense charged at trial—that is, that the defendant ". . . if at large, constitutes a threat of bodily harm to members of the public, or is an habitual offender and mentally ill."[25] Sentencing pursuant to the Sex Offenders Act without the requisite hearing violated the defendant's constitutional right to due process of law.

Relying on *Specht,* the court of appeals in *Bolton v. Harris* also found the District of Columbia mandatory commitment statute constitutionally suspect for failing to provide a hearing on the issue of present mental condition. A verdict of acquittal by reason of insanity signifies only that the jury had a reasonable doubt about the defendant's sanity at the time of the criminal act. Under *Bolton,* a new hearing must be held to determine if the insanity-acquittee's mental condition meets the criteria for involuntary civil commitment. To save the District's mandatory commitment statute from constitutional invalidity, the court construed the statute to authorize temporary detention of the insanity-acquittee for an examination of his present mental condition to determine whether civil commitment is appropriate.

The highest appellate courts in New York,[26] Indiana,[27] Arizona,[28] Wisconsin,[29] Michigan,[30] and New Jersey[31] have used similar reasoning and reached similar results in construing their insanity-acquittal commitment statutes. Mandatory commitment is being supplanted by the requirements of civil commitment procedures and civil commitment criteria.

The civil commitment approach may also solve the problem of release. Several courts have explicitly ruled that the statutes governing the release of civilly committed patients shall likewise govern the release of insanity-acquittees who have been civilly committed.[32]

Decisions requiring equality in release have relied on the United States Supreme Court cases of *Baxstrom v. Herold* and *Jackson v. Indiana*.[33] In *Jackson,* the Court held that subjecting a defendant, mentally incompetent to stand trial, ". . . to a more lenient commitment standard and to a more stringent standard of release than those generally applicable to all others not charged with offenses . . . [denies him] equal protection of the laws under the Fourteenth Amendment."[34] Upon the conclusion of their criminal trials, insanity-acquittees are no longer charged with offenses and have been held to be entitled to the same release procedures and criteria as civil patients. The Indiana Supreme Court extended these equal protection guarantees to such matters as convalescent leave, judicial authority to revoke, terminate, or amend the original commitment order, habeas corpus relief, transfer of veterans to a federal hospital, and hospitalization in the district of the patient's residence.[35]

Use of the civil commitment device following insanity acquittal is appropriate. Nevertheless, problems remain with such an approach. The American Bar Foundation reports that civil commitment statutes

> . . . are so broadly worded that they fail to identify with clarity or precision the type and degree of mental illness for which involuntary hospitalization, with the accompanying deprivation of many personal and civil rights, is justified. The statutory language in this area is almost universally obscure or tautological. . . . [For example] New York law permits hospitalization of a person who is "afflicted with mental disease to such an extent that for his own welfare or the welfare of others, or of the community, he requires care and treatment." Even those statutes which rely on the concept of dangerousness as a justification for hospitalization are in significant aspects vague. In application, such a standard can become as broad as the ingenuity of the person who must apply it allows.[36]

Thus, virtually all insanity-acquittees who would be confined under a mandatory commitment statute could also be confined under a civil commitment statute.

If an individual is confined pursuant to an indeterminate mandatory commitment statute, he must sustain the burden of establishing that an improvement in his condition merits his release. In contrast, the location of the burden of proof in the civil commitment process supposedly gives some protection to those subjected to the process. There, the burden of proof is on the state to demonstrate that detention of a mentally ill person is warranted; it is not on him to demonstrate that detention is unwarranted. "Freedom, in short, is presumptively his, to be taken from him only if exceptional circumstances are proved to exist."[37] If the insanity-acquittee is subjected to civil commitment, he would be entitled to this protection.

However, most civil commitment statutes do not specify the weight of the burden placed on the state, and juries have often been permitted to commit a person upon a mere preponderance of the evidence. Only recently have some court decisions, including one from the Court of Appeals of the District of Columbia, required proof beyond a reasonable doubt that the prospective patient meet the criteria for civil commitment.[38] Due to the stigmatization and the loss of liberty accompanying a civil commitment, consideration should be given to imposing a burden of proof beyond a reasonable doubt in civil commitment proceedings.

A more detailed examination of the criteria and procedures for civil commitment is beyond the scope of this book. It suffices to say that articulation of unambiguous criteria and imposition of criminal process safeguards for civil commitment are being advocated, and to some extent accepted, by courts and legislatures.[39] Even the United States Supreme Court has begun to analyze civil commitment issues and to articulate rights of those involved in this process.[40] As these trends continue, civil commitment is becoming an even more desirable and proper approach to the disposition of persons acquitted by reason of insanity.

A related problem concerns not civil commitment itself, but rather the way in which civil commitment devices are invoked for insanity-acquittees. Some jurisdictions accepting civil commitment have ruled that the insanity-acquittee may be detained temporarily for an evaluation of his present mental condition. The length of these detentions varies though sixty days is not uncommon.

A long evaluation period for insanity-acquittees may be inappropriate. For example, California requires a ninety-day confinement for insanity-acquittees.[41] This period is inconsistent with the initial evaluation period of seventy-two hours prescribed by California law for hospitalization of mental patients generally.[42] If a three-day evaluation is sufficient to determine whether certification for intensive treatment is appropriate for these patients, requiring an additional eighty-seven days for insanity-acquittees is extreme.

Even if a state provides for equal periods of evaluational confinement, the problem is not alleviated if the period is excessive for both.[43] Use of lengthy observational periods for mentally ill people has been criticized as an improper device to allow involuntary treatment without an adjudication of the threshold question of whether they are even civilly committable.[44] The most reasonable solution is to limit the evaluation to a short time, perhaps seventy-two hours, and to apply this limitation to both insanity-acquittees and to others being considered for civil commitment.

The third major problem mentioned above—the conditions of confinement—involves the issue of equalizing treatment for insanity-acquittees and other civilly committed patients.

The practice of confining insanity-acquittees in maximum security wards or hospitals and thus imposing special status on them based solely on their label as insanity-acquittees may be constitutionally impermissible as violating both equal protection and due process. The rationale underlying *Baxstrom* and *Jackson* implies that an insanity-acquitted individual has no special status. If he is to be confined at all, he must be confined pursuant to the procedures and criteria used for any other prospective civil patient. Civilly committed patients are not initially admitted to the maximum security wards or hospitals but are transferred there only after they engage in some dangerous conduct in the "regular" wards. Arguably, to automatically deprive an insanity-acquitted patient of regular ward treatment without requiring any dangerous conduct in a regular ward cannot be constitutionally condoned.

In *Covington v. Harris,*[45] the United States Court of Appeals for the District of Columbia held that a civil patient, confined in the maximum security ward of the District's mental hospital as dangerously mentally ill, could properly petition the court by a writ of habeas corpus to obtain a transfer to a less restrictive ward within the same hospital. Chief Judge Bazelon, writing the opinion of the court, noted that although a mere request for a change of dormitories or for a transfer between substantially similar wards would not sustain a petition for habeas corpus, facilities for the criminally insane

> . . . have, in the past, notoriously rivalled maximum security prisons in the pervasiveness of their restraint upon liberty and the totality of their impositions upon dignity. . . . Thus, there is reason to believe that confinement in John Howard [the maximum security ward] is not normally contemplated for civilly committed patients and entails extraordinary deprivations of liberty and dignity which make it, in effect, more penitentiary than mental hospital, even if it also provides some treatment. . . .
>
> It makes little sense to guard zealously against the possibility of unwarranted deprivations [of liberty] prior to hospitalization, only to abandon the watch once the patient disappears behind hospital doors. The range of possible dispositions of a mentally ill person within a hospital, from maximum security to outpatient status, is almost as wide as that of dispositions without. The commitment statute no more authorizes unnecessary restrictions within the former range than it does within the latter.[46]

Subsequent decisions in the same jurisdiction have specified minimal protective procedures that would extend due process to maximum security transfers.[47]

In 1972, New York enacted legislation[48] that is even more protective of the mental patient's right not to be transferred into maximum security confinement.[49] An individual can be transferred only if he is a "dangerous" patient, defined by the statute as one who

> . . . has committed or is liable to commit an act or acts which, if committed by a person criminally responsible for his conduct, would constitute homicide or

felonious assault or is so dangerously mentally disabled that his presence in the department hospital or school is dangerous to the safety of the other patients therein, to the officers or employees thereof, or to the community.[50]

Prior to transfer, the allegedly dangerous patient is entitled to notice and a court hearing at which he is represented by counsel.[51] If the patient is adjudged dangerous, transfer can be ordered only for a period not to exceed six months. Subsequent orders authorizing retention in maximum security for similar six-month periods require new court hearings and determinations that the patient continues to meet the statutory criterion of dangerousness.

Courts have begun to examine the due process considerations involved in internal prison administration. In *Wolff v. McDonnell*,[52] the United States Supreme Court ruled that a major change in the conditions of a prisoner's confinement requires that minimum due process protections be accorded. Other federal courts have described the substantial and detremental effects of transfers between institutions and have imposed due process safeguards because of those effects.[53] These court decisions justify the requirement of safeguards for reasons that have not as yet been articulated in cases involving mental patients. Increased recognition of the rights of confined mental patients can be anticipated as courts begin to draw obvious analogies between the two groups. Surely, nonconvict mental patients are entitled to no less due process protection than convicts.

Recommendations

I recommend that the legislature adopt the following statutes:

Whenever a defendant is acquitted by reason of irresponsibility, the trial court may[54] *order the prosecutor to commence civil commitment proceedings in accordance with procedures in the mental health code.*

Persons who have been civilly committed following an acquittal by reason of irresponsibility shall be admitted to, treated at, released and discharged from the institution in the same manner and to the same extent as are all others who are civilly committed.

Additionally, because a maximum security ward is functionally distinct from other wards and because placement there decreases treatment potential and increases restraints on personal liberty, every patient should be clearly protected against unjustified transfers. Judicial intervention is necessary to scrutinize the propriety of any proposed transfer to maximum security. Thus, a statutory standard and procedures similar to the New York legislation described above should be enacted.[55] I recommend that the legislature adopt the following statute:

1. Prior to the transfer of any state hospital patient to a maximum security facility [ward or institution], a judicial hearing shall be required and judicial approval shall be obtained. The patient shall receive procedural safeguards including, but not necessarily limited to: Notice of the allegation, right to counsel, right to independent psychiatric assistance,[56] *right to confront and cross-examine witnesses, and the privilege against self-incrimination. The burden of proof that the individual meets the statutory criteria for transfer shall be placed on the state. Additionally, the state shall bear the burden of exploring possible alternatives to transfer.*[57]

2. No patient shall be transferred to a maximum security facility [ward or institution] unless the state proves beyond a reasonable doubt that the patient, while a patient in the hospital, committed an act or acts which have resulted in, or if continued will necessarily result in, serious bodily injury or death to other patients or hospital personnel and that no justification for such behavior existed at the time of the act. Further, the hospital must prove that it has undertaken all reasonable efforts to prevent recurrence of the conduct and that such efforts have failed to deter the patient and that there is reason to believe the patient's injurious conduct will continue or be repeated in the future.

3. No patient admitted to a maximum security facility [ward or institution] shall be retained in maximum security confinement for longer than six months except as authorized by court order granted after notice to the patient and an opportunity to demand a hearing as hereinafter provided.

If the superintendent of the hospital determines that any patient admitted to a maximum security facility [ward or institution] requires retention in maximum security confinement because of dangerous mental illness, the superintendent shall apply within six months of the patient's admission for an order authorizing retention. The patient shall be notified of the application and given an opportunity to demand a hearing. The patient shall be accorded all procedural safeguards accorded at the previous hearing. The standard for retention shall be the same as for initial admission to the maximum security facility [ward or institution]. If the standard is met, the court may order retention of the patient for a period not to exceed six months from the date of the order. Further orders for continued retention may be applied for and ordered as above.

Notes

1. Some statutes provide for commitment to prison, jail, or "the custody of the sheriff." American Bar Foundation, THE MENTALLY DISABLED AND THE LAW 404, rev. ed., Brakel and Rock, eds. (Chicago: University of Chicago Press, 1971).

2. *See* A. Goldstein, THE INSANITY DEFENSE 144 (footnotes omitted) (New Haven: Yale University Press, 1967).

3. *Id.* at 146-54.

4. *Id.*

5. *See* Morris, *"Criminality" and the Right to Treatment*, 36 U. CHI. L. REV. 784 (1969) for a discussion of these various categories of patients; for example, persons found incompetent to stand trial, dangerous civil

patients, defective delinquents, and so forth, whom the author denominates as "mentally ill, non-criminal criminals."

6. Dixon v. Attorney General, 325 F. Supp. 966, 969 (M.D. Pa. 1971).

7. Morris, *supra* note 5, at 790.

8. A. Dukay, M.D., *et al.*, FINAL REPORT OF THE IONIA STATE HOSPITAL MEDICAL AUDIT COMMITTEE 17 (1965). For a more extensive description of "patient activities" as reported in the Ionia Medical Audit, *see* Morris, *Mental Illness and Criminal Commitment in Michigan,* 5 U. MICH. J.L. REFORM 1, 11-13 (1971).

9. Wexler, Scoville, *et al., The Administration of Psychiatric Justice: Theory and Practice in Arizona,* 13 ARIZ. L. REV. 1, 235 (1971). Copyright © 1971 by the Arizona Board of Regents. Reprinted by permission.

10. 1969-70 ARIZONA STATE HOSPITAL, ANN. REP. (Aug. 14, 1970) *as cited in* Wexler, Scoville, *et al., supra* note 9, at 235.

11. Wexler, Scoville, *et al., supra* note 9, at 219-20 (footnote omitted).

12. Memorandum from Herbert L. Packer to Norman C. Lindquist, August 16, 1966, on file with the author. Portions of the Packer Report and subsequent memoranda commenting on the report were published in Morris, *The Confusion of Confinement Syndrome Extended: The Treatment of Mentally Ill Non-Criminal Criminals in New York,* 18 BUFF. L. REV. 393, 425-26 (1969). Reprinted with permission.

13. Memorandum from Herbert L. Packer to Norman C. Lindquist, August 16, 1969, at 8-9.

14. Memorandum from S.W. Morgan, M.D., Superintendent and Medical Director, to E.F. Galioni, M.D., Deputy Director, Division of State Services, October 6, 1966, on file with the author.

15. Memorandum from Herbert L. Packer to Norman E. Lindquist, November 28, 1966, at 1.

16. Memorandum from S.W. Morgan, M.D., to E.F. Galioni, M.D., October 6, 1966, at 4.

17. *Id.* Dr. Morgan's statement is:

> On severe assaultive cases, we will usually consider for release when the patient has been three years without evidence of mental illness and has an acceptable social attitude that would indicate he could get along on the outside without assaultive difficulties.

Quaere: If after three years the person does not have an acceptable social attitude, but he is no longer mentally ill, would Atascadero continue to confine him?

18. *Id.* at 5.

19. 395 F.2d 642 (D.C. Cir. 1968).

20. 383 U.S. 107 (1966).

21. 395 F.2d 642, 647 (D.C. Cir. 1968).

22. 386 U.S. 605 (1967).

23. Specifically, defendant was convicted of taking indecent and improper liberties with a child under sixteen years of age. COLO. REV. STAT. ANN. § 40-2-32 (1963).

24. COLO. REV. STAT. ANN. § 39-19-1 to 10 (1963).

25. COLO. REV. STAT. ANN. § 39-19-1 (1963).

26. People v. Lally, 19 N.Y.2d 27, 224 N.E.2d 87, 277 N.Y.S.2d 654 (1966).

27. Wilson v. State, 259 Ind. 375, 287 N.E.2d 875 (1972).

28. State v. Clemons, 110 Ariz. 79, 515 P.2d 324 (1973).

29. State *ex rel.* Kovach v. Schubert, 64 Wis. 2d 612, 219 N.W.2d 341 (1974), *cert. denied*, 419 U.S. 1130 (1975).

30. People v. McQuillan, 392 Mich. 511, 221 N.W.2d 569 (1974).

31. State v. Krol, _____ N.J. _____, _____ A.2d _____ (Aug. 4, (1975).

32. Bolton v. Harris, 395 F.2d 642 (D.C. Cir. 1968); State v. Clemons, 110 Ariz. 79, 515 P.2d 324 (1973); Wilson v. State, 259 Ind. 375, 287 N.E.2d 875 (1972); People v. McQuillan, 392 Mich. 511, 221 N.W.2d 569 (1974).

33. 406 U.S. 715 (1972).

34. *Id.* at 730 (footnote omitted).

35. Wilson v. State, 259 Ind. 375, 384, 287 N.E.2d 875, 881 (1972).

36. American Bar Foundation, *supra* note 1, at 39 (footnotes omitted).

37. A. Goldstein, *supra* note 2, at 160.

38. *See, e.g., In re* Ballay, 482 F.2d 648 (D.C. Cir. 1973); Lessard v. Schmidt, 349 F. Supp. 1078 (E.D. Wis. 1972), *vacated and remanded for specificity in the order,* 414 U.S. 473 (1974), *judgment modified and reinstated*, 379 F. Supp. 1376 (E.D. Wis. 1974), *vacated on other grounds and remanded*, 421 U.S. 957 (1975); Denton v. Commonwealth, 383 S.W.2d 681 (Ky. 1964). *See also In re* Winship, 397 U.S. 358 (1970) (proof beyond a reasonable doubt required for every fact necessary in juvenile delinquency proceedings). *Cf.* Lynch v. Baxley, 386 F.Supp. 378 (M.D. Ala. 1974); and Dixon v. Attorney General, 325 F.Supp. 966 (M.D. Pa. 1971) where the courts required the evidence be clear, unequivocal and convincing.

39. *Id. See also* Kendall v. True, 391 F.Supp. 413 (W.D. Ky. 1975); Bell v. Wayne County Gen. Hosp., 384 F.Supp. 1085 (E.D. Mich. 1974); State *ex rel.* Hawks v. Lazaro, 202 S.E.2d 109 (W. Va. 1974). *See generally Developments in the Law: Civil Commitment of the Mentally Ill*, 87 HARV. L. REV. 1190 (1974).

In the text at pp. 29-30, *supra*, I proposed an expansion of the irresponsibility test beyond the traditional medical model. If a jurisdiction uses the civil commitment device to confine insanity-acquittees, acceptance of my proposed test will necessitate a reexamination of the appropriateness of civil commitment beyond the medical model currently in use.

40. *See* O'Connor v. Donaldson, 95 S.Ct. 2486 (June 25, 1975), in which the United States Supreme Court held that a non-dangerous, mentally ill individual could not be detained indefinitely without treatment.

41. CAL. PENAL CODE § 1026 (West Supp. 1975). CAL. PENAL CODE § 1026a (West Supp. 1975) provides that no hearing on an application for release of an insanity-acquittee " . . . shall be allowed until the person committed shall have been confined for a period of not less than 90 days . . . ." Further applications for release are not permitted until one year from the date of the hearing on a preceding application. In *In re* Franklin, 7 Cal. 3d 126, 496 P.2d 465, 101 Cal. Rptr. 553 (1972), the California Supreme Court ruled that the required ninety-day confinement period is not violative of due process or equal protection of the laws. The court noted that the ninety-day period is well within the six-month period recommended by the Model Penal Code. MODEL PENAL CODE § 4.08 (Proposed Official Draft 1962).

42. CAL. WELFARE & INST. CODE § 5206 (West 1970).

43. The American Bar Foundation, *supra* note 1, at 47-48, lists temporary or observational hospitalization periods ranging from three to 180 days. Some states provide for indefinite observational confinement.

44. Kendall v. True, 391 F.Supp. 413 (W.D. Ky. 1975); Bell v. Wayne County Gen. Hosp., 384 F.Supp. 1085 (E.D. Mich. 1974); Morris, *Civil Commitment in a Suburban County: An Investigation by Law Students*, 13 SANTA CLARA LAWYER 518, 532-34 (1973).

45. 419 F.2d 617 (D.C. Cir. 1969).

46. *Id.* at 622-24.

47. Jones v. Robinson, 440 F.2d 249 (D.C. Cir. 1971); Williams v. Robinson, 432 F.2d 637 (D.C. Cir. 1970).

48. N.Y. Sess. Laws 1972, ch. 251, § 29.13.

49. In Kesselbrenner v. Anonymous, 33 N.Y.2d 161, 305 N.E.2d 903, 350 N.Y.S.2d 889 (1973), the statute was held to violate the patient's constitutional right to due process. Notwithstanding the procedural protections provided by the statute, a finding that the civilly committed mental patient was "dangerous" resulted in his transfer from a facility administered by the Department of Mental Hygiene to Matteawan State Hospital, administered by the Department of Correction. Because the patient was not charged with nor convicted of a crime, such a result was "constitutionally invidious."

50. N.Y. Sess. Laws 1972, ch. 251, § 29.13(a).

51. Pending the hearing, however, the court was also empowered to

"forthwith order" the transfer of the patient if the transferring hospital was not able to properly care for the patient and the "patient was in need of immediate treatment." *Id.* at (h).

52. 418 U.S. 539 (1974).

53. *See* cases listed in Robbins v. Kleindienst, 383 F.Supp. 239 (D.D.C. 1974).

54. I chose the word "*may*" instead of "shall" because the statute should allow the judge discretion not to order commencement of civil commitment proceedings whenever he believes civil commitment is not warranted. For example, the evidence in a case may lead a judge to conclude that the defendant's mental condition has improved significantly since the commission of the criminal act. Even if a judge decides not to order the commencement of civil commitment proceedings, his decision does not preclude others from petitioning for civil commitment pursuant to the appropriate state statutes.

55. The desirability of this approach is not affected by Kesselbrenner v. Anonymous, 33 N.Y.2d 161, 305 N.E.2d 903, 350 N.Y.S.2d 889 (1973), discussed in note 49, *supra*.

56. If the individual is indigent, this assistance should be paid for by the state.

57. The state must prove that no less drastic alternative, such as increased dosage of tranquilizers, is appropriate to the individual's case.

5 Diminished Responsibility

Distinguishing the Doctrine of Diminished Responsibility from the Insanity Defense

Through the insanity defense, society attempts to distinguish between defendants who are criminally responsible for their actions and those who are completely exculpated from criminal responsibility. Thus, evidence of an abnormal mental condition not amounting to "insanity" as defined in the jurisdiction's test of criminal responsibility is often ruled inadmissible. Such an all-or-nothing conceptualization of responsibility for human behavior has been attacked as not being in accord with psychic reality.[1]

However, in twenty-four states (see Appendix A-6), evidence of abnormal mental condition not amounting to "insanity" is admissible on the question of whether defendant had (or was capable of having) the mental state that is an element of the crime with which he is charged. The doctrine by which this evidence is admitted is known by various names: "diminished responsibility," "partial responsibility," "partial capacity," "diminished capacity," and even "partial insanity." Because of confusion engendered by these labels, some jurisdictions avoid any name for the doctrine. In reality, the doctrine has nothing to do with diminishing the responsibility of a defendant due to *his* impaired mental condition; rather it admits evidence of impaired mental condition in determining whether this defendant had (or was capable of having) the mental state required to find any defendant guilty of the crime charged.[2]

A crime consists of a physical act or omission plus an accompanying state of mind. This state of mind, or mental part of the crime, is variously described as *mens rea,* guilty mind, scienter, or criminal intent. Although both the insanity defense and the doctrine of diminished responsibility focus on the mental part of a crime, they do so in different ways and for different purposes. The insanity defense focuses on the *general* issue of whether at the time defendant acted, his mental abnormality was of such severity, as measured by the jurisdiction's insanity test, that he is to be relieved of criminal responsibility for his actions. Stated with oversimplification, the insanity defense issue is whether at the time he acted, the defendant possessed the mental capacity to commit crimes. The doctrine of diminished responsibility focuses on the *specific* issue of whether at the time the defendant acted, he actually possessed the requisite mental state that is an element of the particular crime charged against him. The diminished responsibility issue is whether at the time he acted, defendant possessed the capacity to have the mental state required as an element of the crime charged against him, or if he did possess such capacity, did he in fact have such mental state.

Arguments For and Against the Doctrine

Statutes specifying that the act be done either "maliciously," "intentionally," or "wilfully" in order for criminal liability to attach require an inquiry into the individual's state of mind at the time he acts. Jurisdictions rejecting the doctrine of diminished responsibility apparently reject such an inquiry on the erroneous assumption that a defendant who fails to establish a complete defense of insanity must have possessed the requisite mental state for the crime charged. In these jurisdictions, absent a complete insanity defense, the basis of criminal liability is a defendant's acts, not his thoughts. If his acts are voluntary, they are held to manifest the intent to bring about the criminal consequences.[3]

Opponents of the diminished responsibility doctrine have pointed to the practical difficulties involved in its implementation. For example, diminished responsibility requires juries to evaluate psychiatric testimony that makes a subtle distinction in the degree of mental impairment that makes the defendant incapable of forming a "deliberate and premediated" intent to kill (as required for first degree murder) but that does not prevent him from having an "intent to kill" (as required for second degree murder). Such an evaluation may be beyond the jury's competence.[4] However, a counterargument may be made that the jury-competence problem is not attributable to the diminished responsibility doctrine but rather to the subtle distinctions drawn in the criminal statutes themselves between the elements of first and second degree murder.

Opponents of the diminished responsibility doctrine assert that it produces compromise verdicts. Thus, a jury divided on whether the defendant charged with murder in the first degree should be found guilty or acquitted by reason of insanity may compromise on the middle ground of diminished responsibility and convict him of the lesser crime of murder in the second degree.[5] In response, defenders of diminished responsibility note that juries engage covertly in a compromise process, that such practice can be viewed as an appropriate individualization of justice, and that recognition of the diminished responsibility doctrine gives a proper sanction to this practice.[6]

One researcher studied the California cases involving diminished responsibility and concluded that the defense is inconsistently applied. Defendants who engaged in criminal conduct under similar circumstances receive substantially different treatment, thereby frustrating the criminal law's attempt to achieve equal treatment for similarly situated defendants.[7] Inconsistent application of the doctrine is said to occur for two reasons:

First, the defending lawyer may not take advantage of potentially helpful evidence on the defendant's state of mind because he is unaware of the precise standard by which his client may be judged. Second, trial judges often cannot determine if the defense was properly raised by counsel and, on the appellate level, there is no established standard by which to review the decision of the trier of fact. Such uncertainty ultimately leaves the jury with little guidance as to whether or not to apply the defense, and hence the jury may be left with an unreasonably broad scope for its intuitive and subjective judgments.[8]

Thus, the author concludes that practical problems with the doctrine involve more than the jury's difficulty in perceiving and evaluating sophisticated and often conflicting psychiatric testimony. In his judgment,

. . . uncertain standards accentuate that difficulty and hence enhance the probability of unequal treatment. . . .

In a broader sense, the inequality is directly traceable to the attempt by the courts to incorporate psychiatric thought and language in the definition of a legal standard for judgment. . . . Until the psychiatric science progresses to a degree of sophistication which would assure precise and universally accepted techniques of diagnosis and treatment, extensive incorporation of psychiatric thought and language in a legal standard does not promise to aid legal judgments without at the same time forfeiting important goals of the legal system.[9]

Another author asserts

. . . that although evidence of mental illness may sometimes be logically relevant to whether a defendant had the state of mind required for the offense, the probative value of such evidence is outweighed by: (1) its complexity; (2) the danger of confusing the jury; (3) the danger of a rule giving such evidence its full evidentiary significance being used as a fiction for unrelated purposes; and, (4) the possibility that even those lacking a given state of mind because of mental illness might respond to the threat of punishment.[10]

He concludes that significant problems of administration and the danger of undue prejudice warrant according less than full evidentiary significance to evidence of mental illness offered to disprove defendant's state of mind.[11]

Support for the diminished responsibility doctrine is already widespread and appears to be increasing. The Supreme Court of Pennsylvania accepted the doctrine in a 1972 decision,[12] stating: "We are persuaded by the almost unanimous voice of professionally recognized authorities that such evidence is competent and in certain circumstances admissible."[13] The court cited cases from other jurisdictions accepting the doctrine, the American Law Institute's Model Penal Code, and twelve books and articles.[14]

In *United States v. Brawner,* the Court of Appeals for the District of

Columbia accepted the doctrine. In the District, as in most states, intoxication (even if voluntary) is a defense to a crime requiring specific intent.[15] Extending diminished responsibility beyond the intoxication cases, the court stated:

> Neither logic nor justice can tolerate a jurisprudence that defines the elements of an offense as requiring a mental state such that one defendant can properly argue that his voluntary drunkenness removed his capacity to form the specific intent but another defendant is inhibited from a submission of his contention that an abnormal mental condition, for which he was in no way responsible, negated his capacity to form a particular specific intent, even though the condition did not exonerate him from all criminal responsibility.[16]

Professors LaFave and Scott, in their treatise on criminal law, assert:

> The logic of the partial responsibility doctrine would seem to be unassailable. The reception of evidence of the defendant's abnormal mental condition, totally apart from the defense of insanity, is certainly appropriate whenever that evidence is relevant to the issue of whether he had the mental state which is a necessary element of the crime charged. Were it otherwise, major crimes specifically requiring a certain bad state of mind would, in effect, be strict liability offenses as applied to abnormal defendants.[17]

The due process clause may constitutionally compel acceptance of the diminished responsibility doctrine. In its dictum, one court asked:

> Can this Court say that it is just to pass upon the guilt and innocence of a defendant without allowing *all* of the evidence available to determine whether he had the mental capacity to commit the crime?[18]

Specific Applications of the Doctrine

In nineteen of the twenty-four jurisdictions accepting the doctrine of diminished responsibility, the doctrine has been used in cases involving a prosecution for first degree murder. In most states, murder is divided into two degrees. First degree murder (other than felony murder) requires an intent to kill accompanied by premeditation and deliberation. "Deliberation requires a cool mind that is capable of reflection, while premeditation requires that the one with a cool mind did reflect—at least briefly—before his act of killing."[19] Absent premeditation and deliberation, a homicide committed with an intent to kill constitutes murder in the second degree. Because premeditation and deliberation are by definition necessary elements of first degree murder, a defendant who is able to introduce evidence of an abnormal mental condition to show that either he did not have the capacity to or he did not in fact premeditate or deliberate before he acted can attempt to convince the jury that only second degree murder was committed.

In eight jurisdictions, the doctrine of diminished responsibility has been used to reduce a crime from murder to voluntary manslaughter. Traditionally, a homicide committed "with malice aforethought" is a murder. Without this essential mental element, the homicide is a manslaughter.

Some authorities assert that diminished responsibility is not an appropriate consideration in deciding whether the crime charged as murder is actually voluntary manslaughter.[20] Generally, voluntary manslaughter consists of an intentional homicide committed in a state of passion engendered by a provocation that would cause a reasonable person to lose his normal self-control. The reasonable person standard provides an *objective* criterion for distinguishing manslaughter from murder. Because that standard presumes a person without serious mental abnormality, a *subjective* evaluation of the actor's mental condition is not relevant to the decision.

However, the Supreme Court of California has ruled that evidence of a defendant's abnormal mental condition is admissible on the issue of malice aforethought. In *People v. Wells,*[21] the defendant claimed he acted on his unreasonable belief that defensive force was required against the victim. The court ruled that evidence of the defendant's mental condition to show he attacked out of an unreasonable fear for his own safety is admissible, for in the court's judgment, such an attack would not be committed with malice aforethought.

An even more expansive use of the doctrine of diminished responsibility on the murder-manslaughter distinction was announced by the Supreme Court of California in *People v. Conley.*[22] In California, manslaughter is defined by statute as "the unlawful killing of a human being, without malice."[23] Generally, courts have held that malice is negated only by a finding of provocation. However, in *Conley,* the court stated: "If because of mental defect, disease, or intoxication, . . . the defendant is unable to comprehend his duty to govern his actions in accord with the duty imposed by law, he does not act with malice aforethought and cannot be guilty of murder . . . ."[24] Because California utilizes the *M'Naghten* test of insanity without the irresistible impulse supplement, the *Conley* case may be viewed as a decision to admit evidence of a defendant's inability to conform—that is, loss of control—for the limited purpose of reducing the crime committed where the restrictive insanity test would not permit complete exculpation.

In *People v. Gorshen*,[25] the Supreme Court of California held that the defendant should be allowed to introduce evidence of mental abnormality to show he did not possess the required mental state for voluntary manslaughter. Under California law, a specific intent to kill is an element of voluntary manslaughter. The *Gorshen* decision created speculation that the doctrine of diminished responsibility would be extended to *any* crime requiring *mens rea* and that this extension might result in complete acquittal of a defendant charged with a crime containing no lesser offense. For example, under such a principle, if the defendant's mental condition negates an intent to steal, he may be entitled to acquittal when the charge against him is larceny or robbery.

If the doctrine of diminished responsibility is limited to reducing first degree murder to second degree murder or to voluntary manslaughter, society would probably be adequately protected from dangerous individuals. The sentences that can be imposed even for these reduced crimes are substantial. However, "[t]he complete acquittal of such offenders would release from state control the very persons society should probably fear most—because their endowments are fewer, because they are more suggestible, more manipulable, more fearful."[26]

In the *Conley* case, the Supreme Court of California clarified, to some extent, its statement in *Gorshen.* If a specific intent to kill is not proven, voluntary manslaughter may be reduced to involuntary manslaughter. Thus, in a California homicide case, diminished responsibility will not lead to complete acquittal.

The question remains of whether a defendant may achieve acquittal in non-homicide cases in a jurisdiction that uses an expansive doctrine of diminished responsibility.[27] Similarly, the question remains of whether the doctrine should be expanded to encompass crimes requiring only a general intent or recklessness or even knowledge.[28] Colorado, which is the one jurisdiction other than California utilizing the doctrine of diminished responsibility with some frequency, has enacted a statute permitting a defendant charged with a specific intent crime to ". . . introduce evidence of his mental condition as bearing upon his capacity to form the required specific intent."[29] Thus, diminished responsibility in Colorado is extended beyond homicides but only to other specific intent crimes.

Recommendation

In its Model Penal Code, the American Law Institute recommends adoption of the diminished responsibility doctrine:

> . . . Evidence that the defendant suffered from a mental disease or defect is admissible whenever it is relevant to prove that the defendant did or did not have a state of mind which is an element of the offense.[30]

The Institute justified its proposal with a brief but persuasive comment.

> Some jurisdictions decline for reasons of policy to accord to evidence of mental disease or defect an admissibility co-extensive with its relevancy to prove or disprove a material state of mind. . . . We see no justification for a limitation of this kind. If states of mind such as deliberation or premeditation are accorded legal

significance, psychiatric evidence should be admissible when relevant to prove or disprove their existence to the same extent as any other relevant evidence.[31]

Although the above comment uses examples of *specific* intent states of mind, the language of the Institute's proposal—section 4.02(1)—is not limited to inquiries concerning specific intent. Whenever evidence of mental condition is relevant to state of mind, it is admissible. Thus, even in a *general* intent crime, evidence of abnormal mental condition is admissible to negate the state of mind required for conviction. In those states where the criteria for civil commitment are mental illness plus dangerousness to self or others, even a broadly stated doctrine of diminished responsibility offers adequate protection to society. These civil commitment criteria are used in an increasing number of states.[32]

I recommend that the legislature adopt the following statute based on the American Law Institute's approach:

Evidence of impairment of the defendant's mental or emotional processes or behavior controls shall be admissible whenever it is relevant to prove that the defendant did not have a state of mind which is an element of the crime charged. Whenever the court or jury finds a defendant not guilty because of such proof, the trial court may order the prosecutor to commence civil commitment proceedings in accordance with procedures in the mental health code.

Notes

1. Diamond, *Criminal Responsibility of the Mentally Ill*, 14 STAN. L. REV. 59, 62 (1961).

2. United States v. Brawner, 471 F.2d 969, 998 (D.C. Cir. 1972). *See also* State v. DiPaolo, 34 N.J. 279, 168 A.2d 401 (1961), *clarified in* State v. Sikora, 44 N.J. 453, 210 A.2d 193 (1965).

3. *See, e.g.,* State v. Johnson, 7 Idaho 269, 275-76, 261 P.2d 638, 641 (1953).

4. In Commonwealth v. Hollinger, 190 Pa. 155, 42 A. 548 (1899), the court stated that to require the jury to make such an evaluation is to require the impossible. *See also* M. Guttmacher, THE ROLE OF PSYCHIATRY IN LAW 47 (Springfield: Charles C. Thomas, 1968), where the author states that the diminished responsibility doctrine requires juries to "answer questions which are . . . by their very nature unanswerable."

5. *See generally* Note, *Partial Responsibility: Adequacy of Present Law,* 43 CORNELL L.Q. 283 (1957).

6. Weihofen and Overholser, *Mental Disorder Affecting the Degree of a Crime,* 56 YALE L.J. 959, 977 (1947).

7. Comment, *A Punishment Rationale for Diminished Capacity,* 18 U.C.L.A. L. REV. 561, 568 (1971).

8. *Id.* (footnote omitted).

9. *Id.* at 570-71.

10. Dix, *Mental Illness, Criminal Intent, and the Bifurcated Trial,* 1970 LAW & THE SOCIAL ORDER 559, 570.

11. *Id.* at 572.

12. Commonwealth v. McCusker, 448 Pa. 382, 292 A.2d 286 (1972).

13. *Id.* at 384, 292 A.2d at 287 (footnote omitted).

14. *Id.* at 384 n.1, 292 A.2d at 287 n.1.

15. American Bar Foundation, THE MENTALLY DISABLED AND THE LAW 394, rev. ed., Brakel and Rock, eds. (Chicago: University of Chicago Press, 1971).

16. United States v. Brawner, 471 F.2d 969, 999 (D.C. Cir. 1972).

17. W. LaFave and A. Scott, HANDBOOK ON CRIMINAL LAW 331 (St. Paul: West Publishing Co., 1972).

18. State v. Shaw, 106 Ariz. 103, 112, 471 P.2d 715, 724 (1970) (emphasis added). In a subsequent case, State v. Andrews, the Arizona Supreme Court reiterated its concern that due process requires acceptance of diminished responsibility. In affirming a conviction, the court stated:

> We would call attention to the fact that in the instant case the defendants were permitted to introduce evidence as to their mental capacity, . . . using this as evidence to negative their ability to form an intent to commit the crime for which they were charged. They were not deprived of due process in the presentation of this evidence.

106 Ariz. 372, 378, 476 P.2d 673, 679 (1970).

19. W. LaFave and A. Scott, *supra* note 17, at 327.

20. *See generally id.* at 328-29.

21. 33 Cal. 2d 330, 202 P.2d 53, *cert. denied,* 338 U.S. 836 (1949).

22. 64 Cal. 2d 310, 411 P.2d 911, 49 Cal. Rptr. 815 (1966).

23. CAL. PENAL CODE § 192 (West 1970).

24. People v. Conley, 64 Cal. 2d 310, 322, 411 P.2d 911, 918, 49 Cal. Rptr. 815, 822 (1966).

25. 51 Cal. 2d 716, 336 P.2d 492 (1959).

26. A. Goldstein, THE INSANITY DEFENSE 202 (New Haven: Yale University Press, 1967).

27. For a discussion of the California cases on the doctrine of diminished responsibility, *see* Comment, *Keeping Wolff From the Door:*

California's Diminished Capacity Concept, 60 CALIF. L. REV. 1641 (1972); Comment, *Diminished Capacity: Its Potential Effect in California,* 3 LOYOLA U.L. REV. 153 (1970).

28. For a discussion of the various mental states required for a crime, *see generally* LaFave and Scott, *supra* note 17, at 191-203. In Rhodes v. United States, 282 F.2d 59 (4th Cir. 1960), the court held that evidence of mental disorder is admissible to prove that defendant did not "knowingly" make false statements on his income tax returns.

29. COLO. REV. STAT. § 16-8-103(1) (1973).

30. MODEL PENAL CODE § 4.02(1) (Proposed Official Draft 1962).

31. MODEL PENAL CODE § 4.02 (1), Comments, at 193 (Tent. Draft No. 4, 1955).

32. A. Brooks, LAW, PSYCHIATRY AND THE MENTAL HEALTH SYSTEM 677 (Boston: Little, Brown and Co., 1974). A number of recent court decisions have imposed a civil commitment standard of mental illness plus imminent dangerousness. *See,e.g.,* Bell v. Wayne County Gen. Hosp., 384 F. Supp. 1085 (E.D. Mich. 1974); Lessard v. Schmidt, 349 F. Supp. 1078 (E.D. Wis. 1972), *vacated and remanded for specificity in the order*, 404 U.S. 473 (1974), *judgment modified and reinstated,* 379 F. Supp. 1376 (E.D. Wis. 1974), *vacated on other grounds and remanded*, 421 U.S. 957 (1975); Dixon v. Attorney General, 325 F.Supp. 966 (M.D. Pa. 1971).

6 Conclusion

In 1972, Mr. Justice Blackmun, writing for the United States Supreme Court, expressed amazement at the paucity of cases involving the states' broad power to confine mentally ill persons:

> Considering the number of persons affected, it is perhaps remarkable that the substantive constitutional limitations on this power have not been more frequently litigated.[1]

Just before this manuscript went to the publisher, the Supreme Court ruled: "A finding of 'mental illness' alone cannot justify a State's locking a person up against his will and keeping him indefinitely in simple custodial confinement."[2] Although these two cases did not involve insanity-acquittees per se, litigation on insanity defense issues is likely as a part of this increased sensitivity toward the rights of the mentally ill. Insanity defense themes can be fully appreciated only in this broader context.

Just as antiquated legislation and practices dehumanized the mentally ill by permitting warehousing of non-dangerous people, existing insanity defense legislation and practices degrade mentally ill people charged with crimes. In reality, the defense is available only to defendants charged with serious crimes that were committed in an extraordinary fashion. These defendants often have no other defense available and are willing to accept indeterminate maximum security mental institutionalization in lieu of long or life sentences in prison. Media accounts of these unusual crimes foster reactions of revulsion and fear. But these exceptional cases and the emotions they engender should not control our judgment on insanity defense issues.

Society can obtain adequate protection from the truly dangerous mentally ill individual without depriving *any* defendant of the opportunity to effectively use the insanity defense to explain his behavior. My recommendations for an improved and expanded insanity test, procedural safeguards in the trial of the insanity defense, psychiatric assistance for the accused in presenting the issue, treatment of the insanity-acquittee as any other mentally ill individual, and increased use of the diminished responsibility doctrine are first steps in implementing rational policies toward mentally ill criminal defendants.

Recent court decisions suggest that the immediate future will be an exciting time for constitutional litigation on the rights of the mentally ill. It would be unfortunate if legislatures—the policy makers in our society—do not become fully involved in passing enlightened legislation to secure these developing rights. As Oliver Wendell Holmes succinctly stated: "[I]t must be remembered that legislatures are ultimate guardians of the liberties and welfare of the people in quite as great a degree as the courts."[3]

Notes

1. Jackson v. Indiana, 406 U.S. 715, 737 (1972) (footnotes omitted).
2. O'Connor v. Donaldson, 95 S. Ct. 2486, 2493 (June 26, 1975).
3. Missouri, K. & T. Ry. v. May, 194 U.S. 267, 270 (1904) (Holmes, J.).

Appendixes

Appendix A
Insanity Defense Issues

Appendix A-1: The Tests of Insanity

Twenty-one states currently apply the *M'Naghten* test of criminal responsibility. This classic right/wrong formulation is imposed as follows:

By statute with supporting case law in three states—Louisiana, Minnesota, and South Dakota;

By case law in eighteen states—Arizona, California, Florida, Iowa, Kansas, Mississippi, Nebraska, Nevada, New Jersey, North Carolina, North Dakota, Oklahoma, Pennsylvania, Rhode Island, South Carolina, Tennessee, Washington, and Wisconsin.*†

In the eleven states listed below, an irresistible impulse test supplements the *M'Naghten* formulation:

By statute in four states—Colorado, Delaware, Georgia, and Hawaii;

By case law in seven states—Alabama, Arkansas, Michigan, New Mexico,* Utah, Virginia* and Wyoming.

The *Durham* test of criminal responsibility is applied in two states:

By statute—Maine;

By case law—New Hampshire.

The ALI Model Penal Code test has been adopted by the seventeen states listed below:

By statute in twelve states—Alaska, Connecticut, Idaho, Illinois, Maryland, Missouri, Montana,* New York,* Oregon, Texas, Vermont, and Wisconsin;*†

By case law in five states—Indiana, Kentucky,* Massachusetts, Ohio, and West Virginia.

Among the ALI jurisdictions, eleven states use the word "wrongfulness" in stating the test:

Alaska, Connecticut, Idaho, Indiana, Massachusetts, Missouri, New York, Ohio, Texas, West Virginia, and Wisconsin.

Six states use the word "criminality" in stating the ALI test:

Illinois, Kentucky, Maryland, Montana, Oregon, and Vermont.

---

*See Appendix B at appropriate state name for explanation.

†This state is listed in more than one subcategory within Appendix A-1.

Table A-1
The adoption of the ALI Model Penal Code test by the Federal Courts of Appeals

Circuit	*Decision*	*§4.01(1)*	*§4.01(2)*
Second	*United States v. Freeman*, 357 F.2d 606 (2d Cir. 1966)	Wrongfulness	Approved
Third	*United States v. Currens*, 290 F.2d 751 (3d Cir. 1961)	Defendant, as a result of mental disease or defect lacked substantial capacity to conform his conduct to the requirements of the law.	Approved
Fourth	*United States v. Chandler*, 393 F.2d 920 (4th Cir. 1968)	Criminality	Approved
Fifth	*Blake v. United States*, 407 F.2d 908 (5th Cir. 1969)	Wrongfulness	Approved
Sixth	*United States v. Smith*, 404 F.2d 720 (6th Cir. 1968)	Wrongfulness	Rejected
Seventh	*United States v. Shapiro*, 383 F.2d 680 (7th Cir. 1967)	Wrongfulness	Unclear
Eighth	*United States v. Frazier*, 458 F.2d 911 (8th Cir. 1972)	Wrongfulness	Approved
Ninth	*Wade v. United States*, 426 F.2d 64 (9th Cir. 1970)	Wrongfulness	Rejected
Tenth	*Wion v. United States*, 325 F.2d 420 (10th Cir. 1964)	Wrongfulness	Unclear
D.C.	*United States v. Brawner*, 471 F.2d 969 (D.C. Cir. 1972)	Wrongfulness	§4.01(2) is rejected as a basis for instruction to jury. Evidence of past criminal or anti-social conduct is admissible as evidence of mental disease if it is accompanied by expert testimony that the characteristics of these actions constitute convincing evidence of an underlying mental disease that substantially impairs behavioral controls.

Although *M'Naghten* is retained as the test of criminal responsibility in the first circuit, the United States Court of Appeals for the First Circuit commended the ALI formulation to the district courts' attention. *Beltran v. United States*, 302 F.2d 48 (1st Cir. 1962).

Appendix A-2: Burden of Proof

In the twenty-six states listed below, the defendant's sanity must be proved by the prosecution beyond a reasonable doubt (the persuasion burden):

> Alaska, Arizona, Colorado, Connecticut, Florida, Hawaii, Idaho, Illinois, Indiana, Iowa, Kansas, Maryland, Massachusetts, Michigan, Mississippi, Nebraska, New Hampshire, New Mexico, New York, Oklahoma, South Dakota, Tennessee, Utah, Vermont, Wisconsin,*† and Wyoming.

In these twenty-six states, the prosecution's ultimate burden to prove insanity beyond a reasonable doubt is fully satisfied by the presumption of sanity and, unless the defendant offers evidence of insanity, there is no requirement that the prosecution present affirmative proof of sanity as a part of its case in chief. Even within individual jurisdictions, the cases are not always uniform in describing the quality and quantity of evidence that the defendant must introduce to deprive the presumption of sanity of its probative effect. To some extent, the differences in language describing the defendant's production burden are semantic only. Nevertheless, cases have been found indicating that the initial production burden is satisfied by introduction of:

> "Some," "any," or "slight" evidence of insanity in eight states—Colorado, Hawaii, Illinois, Indiana, Kansas, Michigan, Nebraska, Utah;
>
> "Evidence" of insanity in eight states—Alaska, Arizona, Kentucky, Massachusetts, New Hampshire, New York, Wyoming, Vermont;
>
> "Sufficient evidence" of insanity in one state—South Dakota;
>
> "Substantial evidence" of insanity in two states—Connecticut and Iowa;
>
> Evidence raising a "reasonable doubt" of defendant's sanity in eight states—Florida, Idaho, Maryland, Mississippi, New Mexico, Oklahoma, Tennessee, Wisconsin.

In the federal courts, the introduction of some evidence of insanity by the defendant places a burden on the government of proving sanity beyond a reasonable doubt. *Davis v. United States*, 160 U.S. 469 (1895).

*See Appendix B at appropriate state name for explanation.

†This state listed in more than one subcategory within Appendix A-2.

In the twenty-five states listed below, insanity is an affirmative defense that must be proved by the defendant by a preponderance of the evidence:

Alabama, Arkansas, California, Delaware, Georgia, Kentucky, Louisiana, Maine, Minnesota, Missouri, Montana, Nevada, New Jersey, North Carolina, North Dakota,* Ohio, Oregon, Pennsylvania, Rhode Island, South Carolina, Texas, Virginia, Washington, West Virginia, and Wisconsin.*†

Appendix A-3: Compulsory Mental Examination

Twenty-six states have specific statutory provisions for a court-ordered mental examination when *either* the issue of the defendant's competency to stand trial or the issue of criminal responsibility is raised:

Alabama (in capital offenses only), Alaska, Arizona, Arkansas, Colorado, Florida, Idaho, Indiana, Kansas, Louisiana, Maine, Maryland, Massachusetts, Missouri, Montana, New Hampshire, North Dakota, Ohio, Oregon, South Carolina, Tennessee, Texas, Vermont, West Virginia, Wisconsin, and Wyoming.

Five states have statutory provisions for a court-ordered mental examination only when the issue of defendant's criminal responsibility is raised:

California, Hawaii, Kentucky (only where two prior felony convictions),* South Dakota, and Utah.

Twelve states have statutory provisions for a court-ordered mental examination only when the issue of defendant's competency to stand trial is raised:

Connecticut, Michigan, Mississippi, Nebraska, Nevada, New Mexico, New York, North Carolina, Oklahoma, Pennsylvania, Rhode Island, and Virginia.

The federal statutes specifically authorize a mental examination only when the issue of defendant's competency to stand trial is raised. 18 U.S.C.A. § 4244 (1969).

Appendix A-4: Instructing the Jury on the Consequences of a Verdict of Not Guilty by Reason of Insanity

In four states, Kansas, New Jersey, Nevada, and Washington,* an instruction is to be given regardless of whether defendant requests it.

*See Appendix B at appropriate state name for explanation.

†This state listed in more than one subcategory within Appendix A-2.

In Michigan, an instruction is to be given only when requested by either the defendant or the jury.

In Massachusetts, an instruction is to be given only when requested by the defendant or when requested by the jury and the defendant does not object.

In Alaska, an instruction is to be given only when requested by the defendant.

In three states, Connecticut, Florida, and Utah,* an instruction is within the trial court's discretion.

In sixteen states, appellate courts have ruled that the defendant has no right to such an instruction whether requested or not:

Arkansas, Delaware, Hawaii, Illinois, Maine, Missouri, New Hampshire, New Jersey, New York, North Carolina, Ohio, Oregon, Pennsylvania, Vermont, Wisconsin, and Wyoming.

Research has not disclosed a resolution of the matter in the remaining states.

Appendix A-5: Confinement of the Defendant upon Acquittal by Reason of Insanity

Seventeen states impose automatic commitment of a defendant determined to be not guilty by reason of insanity:

Arkansas, Colorado, Georgia, Idaho (civil commitment procedure after six months), Kansas, Louisiana (capital cases),† Maine, Maryland (capital cases),† Michigan (examination only),* Minnesota, Missouri, Montana (hearing within 50 days for release),* Nebraska, Nevada, New York (examination only),* Ohio, and Rhode Island (60 days).*†

Nine states require commitment if the judge finds that release would be dangerous to the public:

Alaska, Connecticut,* Florida, Iowa, Louisiana,*† North Dakota, Oregon,† Rhode Island (after 60 day confinement for evaluation),*† and Virginia.

Five states require commitment if the judge finds that the defendant's insanity continues:

Alabama, California, Hawaii, Illinois,† and Oregon.†

Three states require commitment if the jury finds that release would be dangerous to the public:

Mississippi,† Oklahoma, and Washington.*†

---

*See Appendix B at appropriate state name for explanation.

†This state listed in more than one subcategory within Appendix A-5.

Three states require commitment if the jury finds that the defendant's insanity continues:

Illinois,† Mississippi,† and Washington.*†

Two states, Kentucky and Texas, require commitment if a second jury, impaneled after the acquittal, finds that release would be dangerous to the public.

Six states provide for discretionary commitment by the trial judge without specifying the grounds for commitment:

Delaware, Maryland,† Massachusetts, New Hampshire, Pennsylvania, and South Dakota.

Twelve states provide that civil commitment proceedings must be instituted if defendant is to be retained after acquittal:

Arizona, Indiana, Louisiana,*† New Jersey,* North Carolina, South Carolina, Tennessee, Utah, Vermont, West Virginia, Wisconsin,* and Wyoming. (*See also* Idaho,* Michigan,* Montana,* and New York.*)

Appendix A-6: Diminished Responsibility

Twenty-four states have ruled that evidence of abnormal mental condition, although not sufficient to establish legal insanity as a complete defense, is admissible for the purpose of determining which crime was committed:

Alaska, California, Colorado, Connecticut, Hawaii, Idaho, Iowa, Kentucky, Missouri, Montana, Nebraska, Nevada, New Jersey, New Mexico, New York,* Ohio, Oregon, Pennsylvania, Rhode Island, Tennessee, Utah, Virginia, Washington, and Wyoming.

Of these states, nineteen allow the defendant to introduce evidence of an abnormal mental condition for the purpose of showing that a defendant charged with first degree murder did not have the capacity to, or in fact did not, deliberate or premeditate the act at the time the homicide was committed, and that for this reason, only murder in the second degree was committed:

Alaska,* California, Colorado, Connecticut, Iowa, Missouri, Nebraska, Nevada (limited to state of mind but not capacity),* New Jersey, New Mexico, New York, Ohio, Oregon, Rhode Island, Tennessee, Utah, Virginia, Washington, and Wyoming.

Eight states allow the defendant to introduce evidence of an abnormal mental condition to show that defendant either did not have the capacity to,

*See Appendix B at appropriate state name for explanation.

†This state listed in more than one subcategory within Appendix A-5.

or in fact did not, entertain malice at the time of the homicide, and thus is guilty of manslaughter rather than murder:

California, Hawaii, Missouri, Ohio, Oregon, Pennsylvania, Utah, and Washington.

Two states have expressly refused to allow a defendant to introduce evidence of an abnormal mental condition on the issue of malice in a homicide:

Iowa and New Jersey. (*See also* Alaska.*)

Ten states allow the defendant to introduce evidence of an abnormal mental condition to show that when a specific intent is a requisite element of a crime charged, even though the crime is not a homicide, defendant did not or could not have the requisite intent:

California, Colorado, Delaware, Missouri, Montana, Nebraska, New York, Oregon, Texas,* and Washington.

Eight states have ruled that evidence of an abnormal mental condition that does not amount to legal insanity is not admissible for the purpose of proving that the crime charged was not committed or that only a lesser crime than that charged was committed:

Arizona, Arkansas, Florida, Louisiana, Maryland, Massachusetts, West Virginia, and Wisconsin.

Nine states admit evidence of an abnormal mental condition for the purpose of mitigating the punishment to be imposed upon a finding of guilt:

Arizona (capital cases only), Georgia, Idaho, Missouri (capital cases only), New Jersey, Oregon, Pennsylvania, Tennessee, and Texas.

*See Appendix B at appropriate state name for explanation.

Appendix B
State-by-State Analysis

Alabama

The Test: *M'Naghten* supplemented by irresistible impulse. *Lokos v. State*, 278 Ala. 586, 179 So. 2d 714 (1965).

Burden of Proof: On defendant to prove insanity by a preponderance of the evidence. ALA. CODE tit. 15, § 422 (1958).

Psychiatric Exam: Authorized when competency to stand trial or criminal responsibility is raised as an issue and defendant is charged with a capital offense. ALA. CODE tit. 15, § 425 (1958).

Post-Acquittal Confinement: Commitment is required if judge finds that insanity continues. ALA. CODE tit. 15, § 429 (1958).

Alaska

The Test: ALI ("wrongfulness" was the word chosen in the ALI formulation). An abnormality manifested only by repeated criminal or antisocial conduct is not included in the definition of "mental disease or defect." ALASKA STAT. § 12.45.083 (1972).

Burden of Proof: On prosecution to prove sanity beyond a reasonable doubt. ALASKA STAT. § 12.45.083(b) (1972) construed in *Dolchok v. State*, 519 P.2d 457 (Alas. 1974).

Psychiatric Exam: Authorized when competency to stand trial or criminal responsibility is raised as an issue. ALASKA STAT. §§ 12.45.087 (1972), 12.45.100 (Supp. 1974).

Statement to Jury Concerning Effect of Acquittal: Jury instruction to be given upon request of defendant. *Schade v. State*, 512 P.2d 907 (Alas. 1973).

Post-Acquittal Confinement: Commitment is required if judge finds that release would be dangerous to the public. ALASKA STAT. § 12.45.090 (1972).

Diminished Responsibility: Evidence of an abnormal mental condition, although not sufficient to establish legal insanity as a complete defense, is admissible for the purpose of determining which crime was committed. ALASKA STAT. § 12.45.085 (1972).

Evidence of an abnormal mental condition is admissible for the purpose of showing that defendant charged with first degree murder did not have the capacity to, or in fact did not, deliberate or premeditate the act at the time the homicide was committed, and that for this reason, only second degree murder was committed. *Johnson v. State*, 511 P.2d 118 (Alas. 1973). However, the court in its dictum expressed ". . . reservations concerning the applicability of the doctrine of diminished capacity to reduce murder to manslaughter."

Arizona

The Test: *M'Naghten. State v. Shaw*, 106 Ariz. 103, 471 P.2d 715 (1970).

Burden of Proof: On prosecution to prove sanity beyond a reasonable doubt. *State v. Begay*, 110 Ariz. 200, 516 P.2d 573 (1973).

Psychiatric Exam: Authorized when competency to stand trial or criminal responsibility is raised as an issue. ARIZ. REV. STAT. ANN. 1973 Rules Crim. Proc. RULE 11.3.

Post-Acquittal Confinement: Civil commitment proceedings must be instituted if defendant is to be retained after acquittal. ARIZ. REV. STAT. ANN. 1973 Rules Crim. Proc. RULE 25. The civil commitment procedures are found in ARIZ. REV. STAT. ANN. §§ 36-501 through 36-544 (1974).

Diminished Responsibility: Evidence of an abnormal mental condition not amounting to legal insanity is not admissible for the purpose of proving that the crime charged was not committed or that only a lesser crime than that charged was committed. *State v. Janovic*, 101 Ariz. 203, 417 P.2d 527 (1966).

Evidence of an abnormal mental condition is admissible only for the purpose of mitigating the punishment to be imposed upon a finding of guilt in a capital case. *State v. Janovic*, 101 Ariz. 203, 417 P.2d 527 (1966).

Arkansas

The Test: *M'Naghten* supplemented by irresistible impulse. *Stanley v. State*, 248 Ark. 787, 454 S.W.2d 72 (1970).

Burden of Proof: On defendant to prove insanity by a preponderance of the evidence. *Stanley v. State*, 248 Ark. 787, 454 S.W.2d 72 (1970).

Psychiatric Exam: Authorized when competency to stand trial or criminal responsibility is raised as an issue. ARK. STAT. ANN. § 43-1301 (1947).

Statement to Jury Concerning Effect of Acquittal: Defendant has no right to an instruction whether requested or not. *Campbell v. State*, 216 Ark. 878, 228 S.W.2d 470 (1950).

Post-Aquittal Confinement. Commitment is automatic upon acquittal by reason of insanity. ARK. STAT. ANN. § 59-411 (1947).

Diminished Responsibility: Evidence of an abnormal mental condition not amounting to legal insanity is not admissible for the purpose of proving that the crime charged was not committed or that only a lesser crime than that charged was committed. *Bell v. State*, 120 Ark. 530, 180 S.W. 186 (1915).

California

The Test: *M'Naghten*. *People v. Wolff*, 61 Cal. 2d 795, 394 P.2d 959, 40 Cal. Rptr. 271 (1964).

Burden of Proof: On defendant to prove insanity by a preponderance of the evidence. *People v. Kelly*, 10 Cal. 3d 565, 516 P.2d 875, 111 Cal. Rptr. 171 (1973).

Psychiatric Exam: Authorized only when criminal responsibility is raised as an issue. CAL. PENAL CODE § 1027 (West 1970).

Post-Aquittal Confinement: Commitment is required unless the judge finds that defendant has fully recovered his sanity. CAL. PENAL CODE § 1026 (West Supp. 1975).

Diminished Responsibility: Evidence of an abnormal mental condition, although not sufficient to establish legal insanity as a complete defense, is admissible for the purpose of determining which crime was committed. *People v. Nicolaus*, 65 Cal. 2d 866, 423 P.2d 787, 56 Cal. Rptr. 635 (1967).

Evidence of an abnormal mental condition is admissible for the purpose of showing that defendant charged with the first degree murder did not have the capacity to, or in fact did not, deliberate or premeditate the act at the time the homicide was committed, and that for this reason, only second degree murder was committed. *People v. Gorshen*, 51 Cal. 2d 716, 336 P.2d 492 (1959).

Evidence of an abnormal mental condition is admissible to show that defendant either did not have the capacity to, or in fact did not, entertain malice at the time of the homicide, and thus is guilty of manslaughter rather than murder. *People v. Wells*, 33 Cal. 2d 330, 202 P.2d 53 (1949).

Evidence of an abnormal mental condition is admissible to show that when a specific intent is a requisite element of a crime charged, even though the crime is not a homicide, defendant did not or could not have the requisite intent. *People v. Taylor*, 220 Cal. App. 2d 212, 33 Cal. Rptr. 654 (1963).

Colorado

The Test: *M'Naghten* supplemented by irresistible impulse. COLO. REV. STAT. § 16-8-101 (1973).

Burden of Proof: On prosecution to prove sanity beyond a reasonable doubt. COLO. REV. STAT. § 16-8-105(2) (1973).

Psychiatric Exam: Authorized when competency to stand trial or criminal responsibility is raised as an issue. COLO. REV. STAT. §§ 16-8-105(1), 106, 111(1)(2) (1973).

Post-Acquittal Confinement: Commitment is automatic upon acquittal by reason of insanity. COLO. REV. STAT. § 16-8-105(4) (1973).

Diminished Responsibility: Evidence of abnormal mental condition, although not sufficient to establish legal insanity as a complete defense, is admissible for the purpose of determining which crime was committed. COLO. REV. STAT. § 16-8-103(1) (1973). *See also Becksted v. People*, 133 Colo. 72, 292 P.2d 189 (1956).

Evidence of an abnormal mental condition is admissible for the purpose of showing that defendant charged with first degree murder did not have the capacity to, or in fact did not, deliberate or premeditate the act at the time the homicide was committed, and that for this reason, only second degree murder was committed. *Ingles v. People*, 92 Colo. 518, 22 P.2d 1109 (1933).

Evidence of an abnormal mental condition is admissible to show that when a specific intent is a requisite element of a crime charged, even though the crime is not a homicide, defendant did not or could not have the requisite intent. COLO. REV. STAT. § 16-8-103(1) (1973). *See also Schwickrath v. People*, 159 Colo. 390, 411 P.2d 961 (1966).

Connecticut

The Test: ALI ("wrongfulness" was the word chosen in the ALI formulation). An abnormality manifested only by repeated criminal or antisocial conduct is not included in the definition of "mental disease or defect." CONN. GEN. STAT. ANN. § 53a-13 (Cum. Supp. 1969).

Burden of Proof: On prosecution to prove sanity beyond a reasonable doubt. *State v. Dubina*, 164 Conn. 95, 318 A.2d 95 (1972).

Psychiatric Exam: Authorized only when competency to stand trial is raised as an issue. CONN. GEN. STAT. ANN. § 54-40 (Cum. Supp. 1969).

Statement to Jury Concerning Effect of Acquittal: Explanation is within the trial court's discretion. *State v. Wade*, 96 Conn. 238, 113 A. 458 (1921).

Post-Aquittal Confinement: The trial judge may in his discretion order commitment for examination to determine defendant's mental condition. If the court can determine that the defendant is not mentally ill to the extent that he constitutes a danger to himself or others, the court may order his release. CONN. GEN. STAT. ANN. § 53a-47 (Cum. Supp. 1969).

Diminished Responsibility: Evidence of an abnormal mental condition, although not sufficient to establish legal insanity as a complete defense, is admissible for the purpose of determining which crime was committed. *State v. Donahue*, 141 Conn. 656, 109 A.2d 364 (1954).

Evidence of an abnormal mental condition is admissible for the purpose of showing that defendant charged with first degree murder did not have the capacity to, or in fact did not, deliberate or premeditate the act at the time the homicide was committed, and that for this reason, only second degree murder was committed. *State v. Donahue*, 141 Conn. 656, 109 A.2d 364 (1954).

Delaware

The Test: *M'Naghten* supplemented by irresistible impulse. DEL. CODE ANN. tit. 11, § 401(a) (1974).

Burden of Proof: On defendant to prove insanity by a preponderance of the evidence. DEL. CODE ANN. tit. 11, §§ 304 and 401(a) (1974).

Statement to Jury Concerning Effect of Acquittal: Defendant has no right to an instruction whether requested or not. *Garrett v. State*, 320 A.2d 745 (Del. Super. Ct. 1974).

Post-Acquittal Confinement: The trial judge may in his discretion order commitment. DEL. CODE ANN. tit. 11, § 403(a) (1974), construed in *Garrett v. State*, 320 A.2d 745 (Del. Super. Ct. 1974).

Diminished Responsibility: Evidence of an abnormal mental condition is admissible to show that when a specific intent is a requisite element of a crime charged, even though the crime is not a homicide, defendant did not or could not have the requisite intent. DEL. CODE ANN. tit. 11, § 407 (1974).

Florida

The Test: *M'Naghten*. *Anderson v. State*, 276 So. 2d 17 (Fla. 1973).

Burden of Proof: On prosecution to prove sanity beyond a reasonable doubt. *Byrd v. State*, 297 So. 2d 22 (Fla. 1974).

Psychiatric Exam: Authorized when competency to stand trial or criminal responsibility is raised as an issue. FLA. STAT. ANN. Rules Crim. Proc. 3.210(a) & (c) (Supp. 1974).

Statement to Jury Concerning Effect of Acquittal: Explanation is within the trial court's discretion. *McClure v. State*, 104 So. 2d 601 (Fla. 1958).

Post-Acquittal Confinement: Commitment is required if the judge finds that release would be dangerous to the public. FLA. STAT. ANN. Rules Crim. Proc. 3.460 (Supp. 1974).

Diminished Responsibility: Evidence of an abnormal mental condition not amounting to legal insanity is not admissible for the purpose of proving that the crime charged was not committed or that only a lesser crime than that charged was committed. *Ezzel v. State*, 88 So. 2d 280 (Fla. 1956).

Georgia

The Test: *M'Naghten* supplemented by irresistible impulse. GA. CODE ANN. §§ 26-702 & 703 (1972).

Burden of Proof: On defendant to prove insanity by a preponderance of the evidence. *Ross v. State*, 217 Ga. 569, 124 S.E.2d 280 (1962).

Post-Acquittal Confinement: Commitment is automatic upon acquittal by reason of insanity. GA. CODE ANN. §§ 27-1502 & 1503 (1972).

Diminished Responsibility: Evidence of an abnormal mental condition is admissible only for the purpose of fixing the punishment to be imposed upon a finding of guilt. *Woods v. State*, 214 Ga. 546, 105 S.E.2d 896 (1958).

Hawaii

The Test: *M'Naghten* supplemented by irresistible impulse. HAWAII REV. STAT. tit. 37, §§ 703-4 and 703-5 (1968).

Burden of Proof: On prosecution to prove sanity beyond a reasonable doubt. *State v. Moeller*, 50 Hawaii 110, 433 P.2d 136 (1967).

Psychiatric Exam: Authorized only when criminal responsibility is raised as an issue. HAWAII REV. STAT. tit. 37, § 711-91 (1968).

Statement to Jury Concerning Effect of Acquittal: Defendant has no right to an instruction whether requested or not. *State v. Moeller*, 50 Hawaii 110, 433 P.2d 136 (1967).

Post-Acquittal Confinement: Commitment is required if the judge finds that defendant's insanity continues. HAWAII REV. STAT. tit. 37, §§ 711-93 and 711-94 (1968).

Diminished Responsibility: Evidence of an abnormal mental condition, although not sufficient to establish legal insanity as a complete defense, is admissible for the purpose of determining which crime was committed. *State v. Moeller*, 50 Hawaii 110, 433 P.2d 136 (1967).

Evidence of an abnormal mental condition is admissible to show that defendant either did not have the capacity to, or in fact did not, entertain malice at time of the homicide, and thus is guilty of manslaughter rather than murder. *State v. Moeller*, 50 Hawaii 110, 433 P.2d 136 (1967).

Idaho

The Test: ALI ("wrongfulness" was the word chosen in the ALI formulation). IDAHO CODE § 18-207 (1972).

Burden of Proof: On prosecution to prove sanity beyond a reasonable doubt. *State v. Myers*, 94 Idaho 570, 494 P.2d 574 (1972).

Psychiatric Exam: Authorized when competency to stand trial or criminal responsibility is raised as an issue. IDAHO CODE ANN. § 18-211 (1972).

Post-Acquittal Confinement: Commitment is automatic upon acquittal by reason of insanity with civil commitment procedure for determining dangerousness after six months. IDAHO CODE § 18-214 (1972).

Diminished Responsibility: Evidence of an abnormal mental condition, although not sufficient to establish legal insanity as a complete defense, is admissible for the purpose of determining which crime was committed. *State v. Clokey*, 83 Idaho 322, 364 P.2d 159 (1961).

Although the Supreme Court of Idaho announced its acceptance of the above-stated principle in *Clokey*, the court did not discuss nor specifically overrule a history of case law that held such evidence not admissible. *See, e.g., State v. Van Vlack,* 57 Idaho 316, 65 P.2d 736 (1937).

Evidence of an abnormal mental condition is admissible for the purpose of fixing the punishment to be imposed upon a finding of guilt. IDAHO CODE § 18-208 (1972).

Illinois

The Test: ALI ("criminality" was the word chosen in the ALI formulation). An abnormality manifested only by repeated criminal or antisocial conduct is not included in the definition of "mental disease or defect." ILL. STAT. ANN. ch. 38, § 6-2(a) (1962).

Burden of Proof: On prosecution to prove sanity beyond a reasonable doubt. *People v. Hawkins*, 53 Ill. 2d 181, 290 N.E.2d 231 (1972).

Statement to Jury Concerning Effect of Acquittal: Defendant has no right to an instruction whether requested or not. *People v. Givans*, 83 Ill. App. 2d 423, 228 N.E.2d 123 (1967).

Post-Acquittal Confinement: Commitment is required if the trial judge or trial jury finds that defendant's insanity continues. ILL. STAT. ANN. ch. 38, § 1005-2-4 (Supp. 1974).

Indiana

The Test: ALI ("wrongfulness" was the word chosen in the ALI formulation). *Dragon v. State*, 316 N.E.2d 827 (Ind. 1974).

Burden of Proof: On prosecution to prove sanity beyond a reasonable doubt. *Young v. State*, 258 Ind. 246, 280 N.E.2d 595 (1972).

Psychiatric Exam: Authorized when competency to stand trial or criminal responsibility is raised as an issue. IND. STAT. ANN. § 35-5-2-2 (1975).

Post-Acquittal Confinement: Civil commitment proceedings must be instituted if defendant is to be retained after acquittal. IND. STAT. ANN. § 35-5-3.2-1 (1975).

Iowa

The Test: *M'Naghten. State v. Thomas*, 219 N.W.2d 3 (Iowa 1974).

Burden of Proof: On prosecution to prove sanity beyond a reasonable doubt. *State v. Thomas*, 219 N.W.2d 3 (Iowa 1974).

Post-Acquittal Confinement: Commitment is permitted if judge finds that release would be dangerous to the public. IOWA CODE ANN. § 785.19 (Supp. 1975).

Diminished Responsibility: Evidence of an abnormal mental condition, although not sufficient to establish legal insanity as a complete defense, it admissible for the purpose of determining which crime was committed. *State v. Gramenz*, 256 Iowa 134, 126 N.W.2d 285 (1964).

Evidence of an abnormal mental condition is admissible for the purpose of showing that defendant charged with first degree murder did not have the capacity to, or in fact did not, deliberate or premeditate the act at the time the homicide was committed, and that for this reason, only second degree murder was committed. *State v. Gramenz*, 256 Iowas 134, 126 N.W.2d 285 (1964).

However, evidence of an abnormal mental condition is *not* admissible to show that defendant either did not have the capacity to, or in fact did not, entertain malice at time of the homicide, and thus is guilty of manslaughter rather than murder. *State v. Gramenz*, 256 Iowa 134, 126 N.W. 2d 285 (1964).

Kansas

The Test: *M'Naghten. State v. Randol*, 212 Kan. 461, 513 P.2d 248 (1973).

Burden of Proof: On prosecution to prove sanity beyond a resonable doubt. *State v. Chase*, 206 Kan. 352, 480 P.2d 62 (1971).

Psychiatric Exam: Authorized when competency to stand trial or criminal responsibility is raised as an issue. KAN. STAT. ANN. §§ 22-3219(2) and 22-3302(3) (1974).

Statement to Jury Concerning Effect of Insanity Acquittal: The court shall instruct the jury as to the effect of insanity acquittal. KAN. STAT. ANN. § 22-3428(3) (1974).

Post-Acquittal Confinement: Commitment is automatic upon acquittal by reason of insanity. KAN. STAT. ANN. § 22-3428 (1974).

Kentucky

The Test: ALI with irresistible impulse modification ("criminality" was the word chosen in the ALI formulation). An abnormality manifested only by repeated criminal or anti-social conduct is not included in the definition of "mental disease or defect." *Terry v. Commonwealth*, 371 S.W.2d 862 (Ky. 1963).

Burden of Proof: On defendant to prove insanity by a preponderance of the evidence. *Henderson v. Commonwealth*, 507 S.W.2d 454 (Ky. 1974).

Psychiatric Exam: Authorized only for a defendant who has been twice previously convicted of felonies to determine whether his mental condition affects criminal responsibility. KY. REV. STAT. ANN. § 210.360 (1969).

Post-Acquittal Confinement: Commitment is required if a second jury, impaneled in the judge's discretion, finds that defendant is of unsound mind. KY. RULES CRIM. PROC. 9.90(2) (1969).

Diminished Responsibility: Evidence of an abnormal mental condition, although not sufficient to establish legal insanity as a complete defense, is admissible for the purpose of determining which crime was committed. *Mangrum v. Commonwealth*, 19 Ky. Law Rptr. 94, 39 S.W. 703 (1897).

Louisiana

The Test: *M'Naghten*. LA. REV. STAT. ANN § 14:14 (1974).

Burden of Proof: On defendant to prove insanity by a preponderance of the evidence. LA. CODE CRIM. PROC. ANN. Art. 652 (1967).

Psychiatric Exam: Authorized when competency to stand trial or criminal responsibility is raised as an issue. LA. CODE CRIM. PROC. ANN. Arts. 643-645; 650 (1967).

Post-Acquittal Confinement: Civil commitment proceedings must be instituted if defendant is to be retained after acquittal. LA. REV. STAT. ANN. § 28.59 (1969). However LA. CODE CRIM. PROC. Art. 654 (1967) provides for automatic commitment upon acquittal by reason of insanity in a capital case and requires commitment in other cases if the judge finds that release would be dangerous to the public.

Diminished Responsibility: Evidence of an abnormal mental condition that does not amount to legal insanity is not admissible for the purpose of proving that the crime charged was not committed or that only a lesser crime than that charged was committed. *State v. Rideau*, 249 La. 1111, 193 So.2d 264 (1967).

Maine

The Test: *Durham*. ME. REV. STAT. ANN. tit. 15, § 102 (1964).

Burden of Proof: On defendant to prove insanity by a preponderance of the evidence. *State v. Collins*, 297 A.2d 620 (Me. 1972).

Psychiatric Exam: Authorized when competency to stand trial or criminal responsibility is raised as an issue. ME. REV. STAT. ANN. tit. 15, § 101 (1973).

Statement to Jury Concerning Effect of Acquittal: Defendant has no right to an instruction whether requested or not. *State v. Park*, 159 Me. 328, 193 A.2d 1 (1963).

Post-Acquittal Confinement: Commitment is automatic upon acquittal by reason of insanity. ME. REV. STAT. ANN. tit. 15, § 103 (1964).

Maryland

The Test: ALI ("criminality" was the word chosen in the ALI formulation). An abnormality manifested only by repeated criminal or antisocial conduct is not included in the definition of "mental disease or defect." MD. ANN. CODE art. 59, § 25 (1972).

Burden of Proof: On prosecution to prove sanity beyond a reasonable doubt. *Fowler v. State*, 237 Md. 508, 206 A.2d 802 (1965).

Psychiatric Exam: Authorized when competency to stand trial or criminal responsibility is raised as an issue. MD. ANN. CODE art. 59, §§ 23 and 25 (1972).

Post-Acquittal Confinement: The trial judge may in his discretion order commitment. (Commitment is required in capital cases). MD. ANN. CODE art 59, § 24 (1972).

Diminished Responsibility: Evidence of an abnormal mental condition not amounting to legal insanity is not admissible for the purpose of proving that the crime charged was not committed or that only a lesser crime than that charged was committed. *Armstead v. State*, 227 Md. 73, 175 A.2d 24 (1961).

Massachusetts

The Test: ALI ("wrongfulness" was the word chosen in the ALI formulation). *Commonwealth v. McHoul*, 352 Mass. 544, 226 N.E.2d 556 (1967).

Burden of Proof: On prosecution to prove sanity beyond a reasonable doubt. *Commonwealth v. McHoul*, 352 Mass. 544, 226 N.E.2d 556 (1967).

Psychiatric Exam: Authorized when competency to stand trial or criminal responsibility is raised as an issue. MASS. GEN. LAWS ANN. ch. 123, § 15(a) (1969).

Statement to Jury Concerning Effect of Acquittal: Jury instruction to be given only when requested by defendant or when requested by the jury and the defendant does not object. *Commonwealth v. Mutina,* ______ Mass. ______, 323 N.E.2d 294 (1975).

Post-Acquittal Confinement: The trial judge may in his discretion order commitment. MASS. GEN. LAWS. ANN. ch. 123, § 16 (1970).

Diminished Responsibility: Evidence of an abnormal mental condition not amounting to legal insanity is not admissible for the purpose of proving that the crime charged was not committed or that only a lesser crime than that charged was committed. *Commonwealth v. Mazza,* ______ Mass. ______, 313 N.E. 2d 875 (1974).

Michigan

The Test: *M'Naghten* supplemented by irresistible impulse. *People v. Musser*, 53 Mich. App. 683, 219 N.W.2d 781 (1974).

Burden of Proof: On prosecution to prove sanity beyond a reasonable doubt. *People v. Woody*, 380 Mich. 332, 157 N.W.2d 201 (1968).

Psychiatric Exam: Authorized only when competency to stand trial is raised as an issue. MICH. COMP. LAWS ANN. § 767.27a (1967).

Statement to Jury Concerning Effect of Acquittal: Jury instruction to be given upon request of defendant or jury. *People v. Cole*, 382 Mich. 695, 172 N.W.2d 354 (1969).

Post-Acquittal Confinement: Commitment is automatic upon acquittal by reason of insanity. MICH. COMP. LAWS ANN. § 330.2050 (1974). However, in *People v. McQuillan*, 392 Mich. 511, 221 N.W.2d 569 (1974), the Supreme Court of Michigan construed the statute to authorize automatic commitment only for up to 60 days for an examination of the insanity acquittee's present mental condition to consider whether civil commitment is appropriate.

Minnesota

The Test: *M'Naghten*. MINN. STAT. ANN. § 611.026 (1971).

Burden of Proof: On defendant to prove insanity by a preponderance of the evidence. MINN. STAT. ANN. § 611.025 (1963).

Post-Acquittal Confinement: Commitment is automatic upon acquittal by reason of insanity. MINN. STAT. ANN. § 631.19 (1971).

Mississippi

The Test: *M'Naghten. Bean v. State*, 297 So. 2d 903 (Miss. 1974).

Burden of Proof: On prosecution to prove sanity beyond a reasonable doubt. *Myrick v. State*, 290 So. 2d 259 (Miss. 1974).

Psychiatric Exam: Authorized only when competency to stand trial is raised as an issue. MISS. CODE ANN. § 99-13-11 (1972).

Post-Acquittal Confinement: Commitment is required if trial jury finds that acquittee is still insane and that release would be dangerous to the public. MISS. CODE ANN. § 99-13-7 (1972).

Missouri

The Test: ALI (''wrongfulness'' was the word chosen in the ALI formulation). MO. STAT. ANN. § 552.030 (1969).

Burden of Proof: On defendant to prove insanity by a preponderance of the evidence. *State v. Holmes*, 439 S.W.2d 518 (Mo. 1969).

Psychiatric Exam: Authorized when competency to stand trial or criminal responsibility is raised as an issue. MO. STAT. ANN. §§ 552.020 through .030 (1969).

Statement to Jury Concerning Effect of Acquittal: Defendant has no right to an instruction whether requested or not. *State v. Garrett,* 391 S.W.2d 235 (Mo. 1965).

Post-Acquittal Confinement: Commitment is automatic upon acquittal by reason of insanity. MO. STAT. ANN. § 552.040 (1969).

Diminished Responsibility: Evidence of an abnormal mental condition, although not sufficient to establish legal insanity as a complete defense, it admissible for the purpose of determining which crime was committed. MO. STAT. ANN. § 552.030 (1969).

Evidence of an abnormal mental condition is admissible for the purpose of showing that defendant charged with first degree murder did not have the capacity to, or in fact did not, deliberate or premeditate the act at the time the homicide was committed, and that for this reason, only second degree murder was committed *State v. Anderson*, 515 S.W.2d 534 (Mo. 1974).

Evidence of an abnormal mental condition is admissible to show that defendant either did not have the capacity to, or in fact did not, entertain malice at time of the homicide, and thus is guilty of manslaughter rather than murder. *State v. Anderson*, 515 S.W.2d 534 (Mo. 1974).

Evidence of an abnormal mental condition is admissible to show that when a specific intent is a requisite element of a crime charged, even though the crime is not a homicide, defendant did not or could not have the requisite intent. MO. STAT. ANN. § 552.030 (1969).

Evidence of an abnormal mental condition is admissible for the purpose of fixing the punishment to be imposed upon a finding of guilt in a capital case. MO. STAT. ANN. § 552.030 (1969).

Montana

The Test: ALI (modified version: The words ''is unable'' were substituted for ''lacks substantial capacity'' in the ALI formulation). An abnormality manifested only by repeated criminal or anti-social conduct is not included in the definition of ''mental disease or defect.'' MONT. REV. CODES ANN. § 95-501 (1969).

Burden of Proof: On defendant to prove insanity by a preponderance of the evidence. MONT. REV. CODES ANN. § 95-503(a) (1969).

Psychiatric Exam: Authorized when competency to stand trial or criminal responsibility is raised as an issue. MONT. REV. CODES ANN. § 95-505(1) (Supp. 1974).

Post-Acquittal Confinement: Commitment is automatic upon acquittal by reason of insanity but hearing must be held within 50 days to determine the acquittee's present mental condition and whether he may be released without danger to others. MONT. REV. CODES ANN. § 95-508 (Supp. 1974).

Diminished Responsibility: Evidence of an abnormal mental condition, although not sufficient to establish legal insanity as a complete defense, is admissible for the purpose of determining which crime was committed. MONT. REV. CODE ANN. § 95-502 (1969).

Evidence of an abnormal mental condition is admissible to show that when a specific intent is a requisite element of a crime charged, even though the crime is not a homicide, defendant did not or could not have the requisite intent. MONT. REV. CODE ANN. § 95-502 (1969).

Nebraska

The Test: *M'Naghten. State v. Smith*, 190 Neb. 722, 211 N.W.2d 922 (1972).

Burden of Proof: On prosecution to prove sanity beyond a reasonable doubt. *State v. Jacobs*, 190 Neb. 4, 205 N.W.2d 662 (1973).

Psychiatric Exam: Authorized only when competency to stand trial is raised as an issue. NEB. REV. STAT. § 29-1823 (1967).

Post-Acquittal Confinement: Commitment is automatic upon acquittal by reason of insanity. NEB. REV. STAT. § 29-2203 (1964).

Diminished Responsibility: Evidence of an abnormal mental condition, although not sufficient to establish legal insanity as a complete defense, is admissible for the purpose of determining which crime was committed. *Starkweather v. State*, 167 Neb. 477, 93 N.W.2d 619 (1958).

Evidence of an abnormal mental condition is admissible for the purpose of showing that defendant charged with first degree murder did not have the capacity to, or in fact did not, deliberate or premeditate the act at the time the homicide was committed, and that for this reason, only second degree murder was committed. *Washington v. State*, 165 Neb. 275, 85 N.W.2d 509 (1957).

Evidence of an abnormal mental condition is admissible to show that when a specific intent is a requisite element of a crime charged, even though the crime is not a homicide, defendant did not or could not have the requisite intent. *Starkweather v. State*, 167 Neb. 477, 93 N.W.2d 619 (1958).

Nevada

The Test: *M'Naghten. Williams v. State*, 85 Nev. 169, 451 P.2d 848 (1969).

Burden of Proof: On defendant to prove insanity by a preponderance of the evidence. *Phillips v. State*, 86 Nev. 720, 475 P.2d 671 (1970).

Psychiatric Exam: Authorized only when competency to stand trial is raised as an issue. NEV. REV. STAT. § 178.415 (1973).

Statement to Jury Concerning Effect of Acquittal: Jury instruction to be given by trial court regardless of whether defendant requests it. *Kuk v. State*, 80 Nev. 291, 392 P.2d 630 (1964).

Post-Acquittal Confinement: Commitment is automatic upon acquittal by reason of insanity. NEV. REV. STAT. § 175.521 (1973).

Diminished Responsibility: Evidence of an abnormal mental condition, although not sufficient to establish legal insanity as a complete defense, is admissible for the purpose of determining which crime was committed. *Fox v. State*, 73 Nev. 241, 316 P.2d 924 (1957).

Evidence of an abnormal mental condition is admissible for the purpose of showing that defendant charged with first degree murder did not deliberate or premeditate the act at the time the homicide was committed, and that for this reason, only second degree murder was committed. However such evidence is not admissible to show that defendant lacked the *capacity* to deliberate or premeditate. *Fox v. State*, 73 Nev. 241, 316 P.2d 924 (1957).

New Hampshire

The Test: *Durham. State v. Jones*, 50 N.H. 369 (1871).

Burden of Proof: On prosecution to prove sanity beyond a reasonable doubt. *State v. Bartlett*, 43 N.H. 224 (1861).

Psychiatric Exam: Authorized when competency to stand trial or criminal responsibility is raised as an issue. N.H. REV. STAT. ANN. § 135.17 (Supp. 1973).

Statement to Jury Concerning Acquittal: Defendant has no right to an instruction whether requested or not. *State v. Prevost*, 193 A.2d 22 (N.H. 1963).

Post-Acquittal Confinement: The trial judge may in his discretion order commitment. N.H. REV. STAT. ANN. § 651.9 (Supp. 1973).

New Jersey

The Test: *M'Naghten. State v. Maik*, 60 N.J. 203, 287 A.2d 715 (1972).

Burden of Proof: On defendant to prove insanity by a preponderance of the evidence. *State v. DiPaglia*, 64 N.J. 288, 315 A.2d 385 (1974).

Statement to Jury Concerning Effect of Acquittal: The court shall instruct the jury as to the effect of an insanity acquittal. *State v. Krol*, _____ N.J. _____, _____ A.2d _____ (Aug. 4, 1975).

Post-Acquittal Confinement: At the request of the State, the insanity-acquittee may be confined in a mental institution for a period of 60 days for observation and examination. Further detention requires application of civil commitment procedures and the civil commitment standard of dangerousness to self or others. The New Jersey statute, N.J. STAT. ANN. § 2A:163-3 (1952), which required commitment of the insanity-acquittee if the trial jury finds that his insanity continues, was declared to be unconstitutional. *State v. Krol*, _____ N.J. _____, _____ A.2d _____ (Aug. 4, 1975).

Diminished Responsibility: Evidence of an abnormal mental condition, although not sufficient to establish legal insanity as a complete defense, is admissible for the purpose of determining which crime was committed. *State v. Sikora*, 44 N.J. 453, 210 A.2d 193 (1965) (dictum).

Evidence of an abnormal mental condition is admissible for the purpose of showing that defendant charged with first degree murder did not have the capacity to, or in fact did not, deliberate or premeditate the act at the time the homicide was committed, and that for this reason, only second degree murder was committed. *State v. DiPaolo*, 34 N.J. 279, 168 A.2d 401 (1961).

However, evidence of an abnormal mental condition is *not* admissible to show that defendant either did not have the capacity to, or in fact did not, entertain malice at the time of the homicide, and thus is guilty of manslaughter rather than murder. *State v. McAllister*, 41 N.J. 342, 196 A.2d 786 (1964).

Evidence of an abnormal mental condition is admissible for the purpose of fixing the punishment to be imposed upon a finding of guilt. *State v. Sikora*, 44 N.J. 453, 210 A.2d 913 (1965).

New Mexico

The Test: *M'Naghten* supplemented by irresistible impulse (i.e., incapable of preventing oneself from committing the act as a result of disease of the mind). *State v. White*, 58 N.M. 324, 270 P.2d 727 (1954).

Burden of Proof: On prosecution to prove sanity beyond a reasonable doubt. *State v. James*, 85 N.M. 230, 511 P.2d 556 (1973).

Psychiatric Exam: Authorized only when competency to stand trial is raised as an issue. N.M. STAT. ANN. § 41-13-3.2 (1967).

Diminished Responsibility: Evidence of an abnormal mental condition, although not sufficient to establish legal insanity as a complete defense, is admissible for the purpose of determining which crime was committed. *State v. Padilla*, 66 N.M. 289, 347 P.2d 312 (1959).

Evidence of an abnormal mental condition is admissible for the purpose of showing that defendant charged with first degree murder did not have the capacity to, or in fact did not, deliberate or premeditate the act at the time the homicide was committed, and that for this reason, only second degree murder was committed. *State v. Padilla*, 66 N.M. 289, 347 P.2d 312 (1959).

New York

The Test: ALI (modified version: ". . . lacks substantial capacity to know or appreciate either: (a) The nature and consequence of such conduct; or (b) That such conduct was wrong.") N.Y. PENAL LAW § 30.05(1) (McKinney 1975).

Burden of Proof: On prosecution to prove sanity beyond a reasonable doubt. *People v. Silver*, 33 N.Y.2d 475, 310 N.E.2d 520, 354 N.Y.S.2d 915 (1974).

Psychiatric Exam: Authorized only when competency to stand trial is raised as an issue. N.Y. CRIM. PROC. LAW § 730.30(1) (McKinney 1971).

Statement to Jury Concerning Effect of Acquittal: Defendant has no right to an instruction whether requested or not. *People v. Adams*, 26 N.Y.2d 129, 257 N.E.2d 610, 309 N.Y.S.2d 145 (1970).

Post-Acquittal Confinement: Commitment is automatic upon acquittal by reason of insanity. N.Y. CRIM PROC. LAW § 330.20 (McKinney 1971). However, in *People v. Lally*, 19 N.Y.2d 27, 224 N.E.2d 87, 277 N.Y.S.2d 654 (1966), the New York Court of Appeals construed the statute to authorize automatic commitment only for an examination of the insanity acquittee's present mental condition to consider whether civil commitment is appropriate.

Diminished Responsibility: Evidence of an abnormal mental condition, although not sufficient to establish legal insanity as a complete defense, is admissible for the purpose of determining which crime was committed. *People v. Moran*, 249 N.Y. 179, 163 N.E. 553 (1928), followed in *People v. Colavecchio*, 11 App. Div. 2d 161, 202 N.Y.S.2d 119 (4th Dep't 1960).

Although the New York Court of Appeals announced its acceptance of the above-stated principle in *Moran*, the court did not discuss or specifically overrule previous New York cases that held such evidence not admissible. *See, e.g., Sindram v. People*, 88 N.Y. 196 (1882).

Evidence of an abnormal mental condition is admissible for the purpose of showing that the defendant charged with first degree murder did not have the capacity to, or in fact did not, deliberate or premeditate the act at the time the homicide was committed, and that for this reason, only second degree murder was committed. *People v. Moran*, 249 N.Y. 179, 163 N.E. 553 (1928).

Evidence of an abnormal mental condition is admissible to show that when a specific intent is a requisite element of a crime charged, even though the crime is not a homicide, defendant did not or could not have the requisite intent. *People v. Colavecchio*, 11 App. Div. 2d 161, 202 N.Y.S.2d 119 (4th Dep't 1960).

North Carolina

The Test: *M'Naghten. State v. Humphrey*, 283 N.C. 570, 196 S.E.2d 516 (1973).

Burden of Proof: On defendant to prove insanity by a preponderance of the evidence. *State v. Hicks*, 269 N.C. 762, 153 S.E.2d 488 (1967).

Psychiatric Exam: Authorized only when competency to stand trial is raised as an issue. N.C. GEN. STAT. § 122-91 (1974).

Statement to Jury Concerning Effect of Acquittal: Defendant has no right to an instruction whether requested or not. *State v. Bracy*, 215 N.C. 248, 1 S.E.2d 891 (1939).

Post-Acquittal Confinement: Civil commitment proceedings must be instituted if defendant is to be retained after acquittal. N.C. GEN. STAT. § 122.84.1 (1974 Sess. Laws, ch. 1437, § 1).

North Dakota

The Test: *M'Naghten. State v. Throndson*, 49 N.D. 348, 191 N.W. 628 (1922).

Burden of Proof: N.D. CENT. CODE § 12-02-01 (1969) *may* place the burden of proof on defendant to prove insanity by a preponderance of the evidence by providing that "upon proof" of insanity, the defendant is deemed incapable of committing crime.

Psychiatric Exam: Authorized when competency to stand trial or criminal responsibility is raised as an issue. N.D. CENT. CODE §§ 29-20-01 and 29-20-03 (1969).

Post-Acquittal Confinement: Commitment is permitted if judge finds that release would be dangerous to the public. N.D. CENT. CODE § 12-05-03 (1969).

Ohio

The Test: ALI ("wrongfulness" was the word chosen in the ALI formulation). *State v. Staten*, 25 Ohio St. 2d 107, 267 N.E.2d 122 (1971).

Burden of Proof: On defendant to prove insanity by a preponderance of the evidence. *State v. Staten*, 25 Ohio St. 2d 107, 267 N.E.2d 122 (1971).

Psychiatric Exam: Authorized when competency to stand trial or criminal responsibility is raised as an issue. OHIO REV. CODE ANN. § 2945.40 (1974).

Statement to Jury Concerning Effect of Acquittal: Defendant has no right to an instruction whether requested or not. *State v. Siddle*, 28 Ohio St. 2d 135, 276 N.E.2d 641 (1971).

Post-Acquittal Confinement: Commitment is automatic upon acquittal by reason of insanity. OHIO REV. CODE ANN. § 2945.39 (1969).

Diminished Responsibility: Evidence of an abnormal mental condition, although not sufficient to establish legal insanity as a complete defense, is admissible for the purpose of determining which crime was committed. *State v. Nichols*, 3 Ohio App. 2d 182, 209 N.E.2d 750 (1965).

Evidence of an abnormal mental condition is admissible for the purpose of showing that defendant charged with first degree murder did not have the capacity to, or in fact did not, deliberate or premediate the act at the time the homicide was committed, and that for this reason, only second degree murder was committed. *State v. Adin*, 7 Ohio Dec. Reprint 25 (C.P. Cuyahoga 1876).

Evidence of an abnormal mental condition is admissible to show that defendant either did not have the capacity to, or in fact did not, entertain malice at time of the homicide, and thus is guilty of manslaughter rather than murder. *State v. Nichols*, 3 Ohio App. 2d 182, 209 N.E.2d 750 (1965).

Oklahoma

The Test: *M'Naghten*. *Hair v. State*, 532 P.2d 72 (Okla. Crim. 1974).

Burden of Proof: On prosecution to prove sanity beyond a reasonable doubt. *Gonzales v. State*, 388 P.2d 312 (Okla. 1964).

Psychiatric Exam: Authorized only when competency to stand trial is raised as an issue. OKLA. STAT. ANN. tit. 22, § 1171 (Supp. 1974).

Post-Acquittal Confinement: Commitment is required if trial jury finds that release would be dangerous to the public. OKLA. STAT. ANN. tit. 22, § 1161 (1958).

Oregon

The Test: ALI ("criminality" was the word chosen in the ALI formulation). An abnormality manifested only by repeated criminal or antisocial conduct is not included in the definition of "mental disease or defect." ORE. REV. STAT. § 161.295 (Supp. 1973).

Burden of Proof: On defendant to prove insanity by a prèponderance of the evidence. ORE. REV. STAT. §§ 161.055(2) and 161.305 (Supp. 1973).

Psychiatric Exam: Authorized when competency to stand trial or criminal responsibility is raised as an issue. ORE. REV. STAT. §§ 161.315 and 161.360 (Supp. 1973).

Statement to Jury Concerning Effect of Acquittal: Defendant has no right to an instruction whether requested or not. *State v. Daley*, 54 Ore. 514, 103 P. 502 (1909).

Post-Acquittal Confinement: Commitment is required if the judge finds that release would be dangerous to the defendant or to the public and that defendant's insanity continues. ORE. REV. STAT. § 161.340 (Supp. 1973).

Diminished Responsibility: Evidence of an abnormal mental condition, although not sufficient to establish legal insanity as a complete defense, is admissible for the purpose of determining which crime was committed. ORE. REV. STAT § 161.300 (Supp. 1973).

Evidence of an abnormal mental condition is admissible for the purpose of showing that defendant charged with first degree murder did not have the capacity to, or in fact did not, deliberate or premeditate the act at the time the homicide was committed, and that for this reason, only second degree murder was committed. *State v. Wallace*, 170 Ore. 60, 131 P.2d 222 (1942).

Evidence of an abnormal mental condition is admissible to show that defendant either did not have the capacity to, or in fact did not, entertain malice at time of the homicide, and thus is guilty of manslaughter rather than murder. *State v. Schleigh*, 210 Ore. 155, 310 P.2d 341 (1957).

Evidence of an abnormal mental condition is admissible to show that when a specific intent is a requisite element of a crime charged, even though the crime is not a homicide, defendant did not or could not have the requisite intent. ORE. REV. STAT. § 161.300 (Supp. 1973).

Evidence of an abnormal mental condition is admissible for the purpose of fixing the punishment to be imposed upon a finding of guilt. *State v. Wallace*, 170 Ore. 60, 131 P.2d 222 (1942).

Pennsylvania

The Test: *M'Naghten. Commonwealth v. Hamilton*, 329 A.2d 212 (Pa. 1974).

Burden of Proof: On defendant to prove insanity by a preponderance of the evidence. *Commonwealth v. Updegrove*, 413 Pa. 599, 198 A.2d 534 (1964).

Psychiatric Exam: Authorized only when competency to stand trial is raised as an issue. PA. STAT. ANN. tit. 50, §§ 4407-4409 (1969).

Statement to Jury Concerning Effect of Acquittal: Defendant has no right to an instruction whether requested or not. *Commonwealth v. Gable*, 323 Pa. 449, 187 A. 393 (1936).

Post-Acquittal Confinement: The trial judge may in his discretion order commitment. PA. STAT, ANN. tit. 19, § 1351 (1969).

Diminished Responsibility: Evidence of an abnormal mental condition, although not sufficient to establish legal insanity as a complete defense, is admissible for the purpose of determining which crime was committed. *Commonwealth v. McCusker*, 448 Pa. 382, 292 A.2d 286 (1972).

Evidence of an abnormal mental condition is admissible to show that defendant either did not have the capacity to, or in fact did not, entertain malice at time of the homicide, and thus is guilty of manslaughter rather than murder. *Commonwealth v. McCusker*, 448 Pa. 382, 292 A.2d 286 (1972).

Evidence of an abnormal mental condition is admissible for the purpose of fixing punishment to be imposed upon a finding of guilt. *Commonwealth v. Ahearn*, 421 Pa. 311, 218 A.2d 561 (1966).

Rhode Island

The Test: *M'Naghten. State v. Nault*, 314 A.2d 627 (R.I. 1974).

Burden of Proof: On defendant to prove insanity by a preponderance of the evidence. *State v. Nault*, 314 A.2d 627 (R.I. 1974).

Psychiatric Exam: Authorized only when competency to stand trial is raised as an issue. R.I. GEN. LAWS ANN. § 26-4-3(4)(b) (Supp. 1974).

Post-Acquittal Confinement: Commitment is automatic for up to 60 days to determine whether the insanity-acquittee is dangerous. Thereafter, if the judge finds that he is dangerous, commitment is required. R.I. GEN. LAWS ANN. § 26-4-4 (Supp. 1974).

Diminished Responsibility: Evidence of an abnormal mental condition, although not sufficient to establish legal insanity as a complete defense, is admissible for the purpose of determining which crime was committed. *State v. Fenik*, 45 R.I. 309, 121 A. 218 (1923).

Evidence of an abnormal mental condition is admissible for the purpose of showing that defendant charged with first degree murder did not have the capacity to, or in fact did not, deliberate or premeditate the act at the time the homicide was committed, and that for this reason, only second degree murder was committed. *State v. Fenik*, 45 R.I. 309, 121 A. 218 (1923).

South Carolina

The Test: *M'Naghten. State v. Cannon*, 260 S.C. 537, 197 S.E.2d 678 (1973).

Burden of Proof: On defendant to prove insanity by a preponderance of the evidence. *State v. Hinson*, 253 S.C. 607, 172 S.E.2d 548 (1970).

Psychiatric Exam: Authorized when competency to stand trial or criminal responsibility is raised as an issue. S.C. CODE ANN. § 32-977 (Cum. Supp. 1974).

Post-Acquittal Confinement: Civil commitment proceedings must be instituted if defendant is to be retained after acquittal. S.C. CODE ANN. § 32-980 (Cum. Supp. 1974).

South Dakota

The Test: *M'Naghten*. S.D. COMPILED LAWS ANN. § 22-3-1 (1967).

Burden of Proof: On prosecution to prove sanity beyond a reasonable doubt. *State v. Kindvall*, 86 S.D. 91, 191 N.W.2d 289 (1971).

Psychiatric Exam: Authorized only when criminal responsibility is raised as an issue. S.D. COMPILED LAWS ANN. § 23-37-2 (1967).

Post-Acquittal Confinement: The trial judge may in his discretion order commitment. S.D. COMPILED LAWS ANN. § 23-45-21 (1967).

Tennessee

The Test: *M'Naghten. Spurlock v. State*, 212 Tenn. 132, 368 S.W.2d 299 (1963).

Burden of Proof: On prosecution to prove sanity beyond a reasonable doubt. *Collins v. State*, 506 S.W.2d 179 (Tenn. Crim. App. 1973).

Psychiatric Exam: Authorized when competency to stand trial or criminal responsibility is raised as an issue. TENN. CODE ANN. § 33-708 (Supp. 1974).

Post-Acquittal Confinement: Civil commitment proceedings must be instituted if defendant is to be retained after acquittal. TENN. CODE ANN. § 33-709 (Supp. 1974).

Diminished Responsibility: Evidence of an abnormal mental condition, although not sufficient to establish legal insanity as a complete defense, is admissible for the purpose of determining which crime was committed. *Covey v. State*, 504 S.W.2d 387 (Tenn. Crim. App. 1973).

Evidence of an abnormal mental condition is admissible for the purpose of showing that defendant charged with first degree murder did not have the capacity to, or in fact did not, deliberate or premeditate the act at the time the homicide was committed, and that for this reason, only second degree murder was committed. *Covey v. State*, 504 S.W.2d 387 (Tenn. Crim. App. 1973).

Evidence of an abnormal mental condition is admissible for the purpose of fixing the punishment to be imposed upon a finding of guilt. *Woodruff v. State*, 164 Tenn. 530, 51 S.W.2d 843 (1932).

Texas

The Test: ALI ("wrongfulness" was the word chosen in the ALI formulation). An abnormality manifested only by repeated criminal or antisocial conduct is not included in the definition of "mental disease or defect." TEX. PENAL CODE § 8.01 (1974).

Burden of Proof: On the defendant to prove insanity by a preponderance of the evidence. *Breland v. State*, 489 S.W.2d 623 (Tex. Crim. App. 1973).

Psychiatric Exam: Authorized when competency to stand trial or criminal responsibility is raised as an issue. TEX. CODE CRIM. PRO. Art. 46.02 § 2(f)(1) (Supp. 1974).

Post-Acquittal Confinement: Commitment is required if a second jury finds that person continues to be insane, i.e., that his mental condition is such that release would be dangerous to the public and to the person. TEX. CODE CRIM. PRO. Art. 46.02 § 3(d)(4) (Supp. 1974).

Diminished Responsibility: Evidence of an abnormal mental condition is admissible to show that when a specific intent is a requisite element of a crime charged defendant did not or could not have the requisite intent. However, such evidence is not admissible where the crime charged is not a crime requiring a specific intent. *Cowles v. State*, 510 S.W.2d 608 (Tex. Crim. App. 1974).

Evidence of an abnormal mental condition is admissible for the purpose of fixing the punishment to be imposed upon a finding of guilt. *Thomas v. State*, 97 Tex. Crim. 432, 262 S.W. 84 (1924).

Utah

The Test: *M'Naghten* supplemented by irresistible impulse. *State v. Holt*, 22 Utah 2d 109, 449 P.2d 119 (1969).

Burden of Proof: On prosecution to prove sanity beyond a reasonable doubt. *State v. Holt*, 22 Utah 2d 109, 449 P.2d 119 (1969).

Psychiatric Exam: Authorized only when criminal responsibility is raised as an issue. UTAH CODE ANN. § 77-24-17 (1953).

Statement to Jury Concerning Effect of Acquittal: Failure to instruct that civil commitment proceedings could be instituted to confine an insanity-acquittee is not prejudicial error. *State v. Kirkham*, 7 Utah 2d 108, 319 P.2d 859 (1958).

Post-Acquittal Confinement: Civil commitment proceedings must be instituted if defendant is to be retained after acquittal. *State v. Kirkham*, 7 Utah 2d 108, 319 P.2d 859 (1958).

Diminished Responsibility: Evidence of an abnormal mental condition, although not sufficient to establish legal insanity as a complete defense, is admissible for the purpose of determining which crime was committed. *State v. Green*, 78 Utah 580, 6 P.2d 177 (1931).

Evidence of an abnormal mental condition is admissible for the purpose of showing that defendant charged with first degree murder did not have the capacity to, or in fact did not, deliberate or premeditate the act at the time the homicide was committed, and that for this reason, only second degree murder was committed. *State v. Green*, 78 Utah 580, 6 P.2d 177 (1931).

Evidence of an abnormal mental condition is admissible to show that defendant either did not have the capacity to, or in fact did not, entertain malice at time of the homicide, and thus is guilty of manslaughter rather than murder. *State v. Green*, 78 Utah 580, 6 P.2d 177 (1931).

Vermont

The Test: ALI (''criminality'' was the word chosen in the ALI formulation). An abnormality manifested only by repeated criminal or anti-social conduct is not included in the definition of ''mental disease or defect.'' VT. STAT. ANN. tit. 13 § 4801 (1974).

Burden of Proof: On prosecution to prove sanity beyond a reasonable doubt. *State v. Bishop*, 128 Vt. 221, 260 A.2d 393 (1969).

Psychiatric Exam: Authorized when competency to stand trial or criminal responsibility is raised as an issue. VT. STAT. ANN. tit. 13, § 4814 (1974).

Statement to Jury Concerning Effect of Acquittal: Defendant has no right to an instruction whether requested or not. *State v. Hood*, 123 Vt. 273, 187 A.2d 499 (1963).

Post-Acquittal Confinement: Civil commitment proceedings must be instituted if defendant is to be retained after acquittal. VT. STAT. ANN. tit. 13, §§ 4820 through 4822 (1974).

Virginia

The Test: *M'Naghten* supplemented by a modified irresistible impulse test. The irresistible impulse doctrine is applicable only when defendant has the capacity to distinguish right from wrong (i.e., a showing of such capacity is a prerequisite). *Davis v. Commonwealth*, 214 Va. 681, 204 S.E.2d 272 (1974).

Burden of Proof: On defendant to prove insanity by a preponderance of the evidence. *Taylor v. Commonwealth*, 208 Va. 316, 157 S.E.2d 185 (1967).

Psychiatric Exam: Authorized only when competency to stand trial is raised as an issue. VA. CODE ANN. § 19.1-228 (Supp. 1975).

Post-Acquittal Confinement: Commitment is required if judge finds that release would be dangerous to the public or that insanity continues. VA. CODE ANN. § 19.1-239(1) (Supp. 1975).

Diminished Responsibility: Evidence of an abnormal mental condition, although not sufficient to establish legal insanity as a complete defense, is admissible for the purpose of determining which crime was committed. *Dejarnette v. Commonwealth*, 75 Va. 867 (1881).

Evidence of an abnormal mental condition is admissible for the purpose of showing that defendant charged with first degree murder did not have the capacity to, or in fact did not, deliberate or premeditate the act at the time the homicide was committed, and that for this reason, only second degree murder was committed. *Dejarnette v. Commonwealth*, 75 Va. 867 (1881).

Washington

The Test: *M'Naghten. State v. Ferrick*, 81 Wash. 2d 942, 506 P.2d 860 (1973).

Burden of Proof: On defendant to prove insanity by a preponderance of the evidence. *State v. Canaday*, 79 Wash. 2d 647, 488 P.2d 1064 (1971).

Statement to Jury Concerning Effect of Acquittal: The court instructs the jury that if it acquits defendant because of insanity, it shall also find: ". . . (3) whether the insanity or mental irresponsibility continues and exists at the time of the trial, and (4) whether, if such condition of insanity or mental irresponsibility does not exist at the time of the trial, there is such likelihood of a relapse or recurrence of the insane or mental irresponsible condition, that the defendant is not a safe person to be at large." WASH REV. CODE ANN. § 10.76.030 (1957).

Post-Acquittal Confinement: Commitment is required if the trial jury finds that defendant's insanity ". . . still exists, or, if it does not exist, that he is so liable to the relapse or recurrence of the insane or mentally irresponsible condition as to be an unsafe person to be at large . . . ." WASH. REV. CODE ANN. § 10.76.040 (1957).

Diminished Responsibility: Evidence of an abnormal mental condition, although not sufficient to establish legal insanity as a complete defense, is admissible for the purpose of determining which crime was committed. *State v. Ferrick*, 81 Wash. 2d 942, 506 P.2d 860 (1973).

Evidence of an abnormal mental condition is admissible for the purpose of showing that defendant charged with first degree murder did not have the capacity to, or in fact did not, deliberate or premeditate the act at the time the homicide was committed, and that for this reason, only second degree murder was committed. *State v. Ferrick*, 81 Wash. 2d 942, 506 P.2d 860 (1973).

Evidence of an abnormal mental condition is admissible to show that defendant either did not have the capacity to, or in fact did not, entertain malice at the time of the homicide, and thus is guilty of manslaughter rather than murder. *State v. Ferrick*, 81 Wash. 2d 942, 506 P.2d 860 (1973).

Evidence of an abnormal mental condition is admissible to show that when a specific intent is a requisite element of a crime charged, even though the crime is not a homicide, defendant did not or could not have the requisite intent. *State v. Carter*, 5 Wash. App. 802, 490 P.2d 1346 (1971).

West Virginia

The Test: ALI ("wrongfulness" was the word chosen in the ALI formulation). *State v. Grimm*, 195 S.E.2d 637 (W. Va. 1973).

Burden of Proof: On defendant to prove insanity by a preponderance of the evidence. *State v. Grimm*, 195 S.E. 2d 637 (W. Va. 1973).

Psychiatric Exam: Authorized when competency to stand trial or criminal responsibility is raised as an issue. W. VA. CODE ANN. § 27-6A-1 (Supp. 1974).

Post-Acquittal Confinement: The trial judge may in his discretion order commitment for examination not to exceed forty days. Civil commitment proceedings may be instituted if defendant is to be retained thereafter. W. VA. CODE ANN. § 27-6A-3 (Supp. 1974).

Diminished Responsibility: Evidence of an abnormal mental condition not amounting to legal insanity is not admissible for the purpose of proving that the crime charged was not committed or that only a lesser crime than that charged was committed. *State v. Flint*, 142 W. Va. 509, 96 S.E.2d 677 (1957).

Wisconsin

The Test: ALI ("wrongfulness" was the word chosen in the ALI formulation). An abnormality manifested only by repeated criminal or antisocial conduct is not included in the definition of "mental disease or defect." WIS. STAT. ANN. § 971.15 (1971). However, defendant has the option to choose *M'Naghten*. *Schleisner v. State*, 58 Wis. 2d 605, 207 N.W.2d 636 (1973); *State v. Shoffner*, 31 Wis. 2d 412, 143 N.W.2d 458 (1966).

Burden of Proof: On defendant to prove insanity by a preponderance of the evidence if defendant chooses ALI test. WIS. STAT. ANN. § 971.15 (1971).

On prosecution to prove sanity beyond a reasonable doubt if defendant chooses *M'Naghten* test. *State v. Shoffner*, 31 Wis. 2d 412, 143 N.W.2d 458 (1966).

Psychiatric Exam: Authorized when competency to stand trial or criminal responsibility is raised as an issue. WIS. STAT. ANN. §§ 971.14 and 971.16 (1971).

Statement to Jury Concerning Effect of Acquittal: Defendant has no right to an instruction whether requested or not. *Simpson v. State*, 62 Wis. 2d 605, 215 N.W.2d 435 (1974).

Post-Acquittal Confinement: Commitment is automatic upon acquittal by reason of insanity. WIS. STAT. ANN. § 971.17 (1971). However, this statute was declared unconstitutional as denying due process and equal protection of the law. *State ex rel. Kovach v. Schubert*, 64 Wis. 2d 612, 219 N.W.2d 341 (1974). Upon acquittal by reason of insanity the jury will be asked to determine if defendant is presently mentally ill and if he is a proper subject for custody and treatment under the state's civil commitment statutes.

Diminished Responsibility: Evidence of an abnormal mental condition not amounting to legal insanity is not admissible for the purpose of proving that the crime charged was not committed or that only a lesser crime than that charged was committed. *Sprague v. State*, 52 Wis. 2d 89, 187 N.W.2d 784 (1971).

Wyoming

The Test: *M'Naghten* supplemented by irresistible impulse. *Reilly v. State*, 496 P.2d 899 (Wyo. 1972).

Burden of Proof: On prosecution to prove sanity beyond a reasonable doubt. WYO. STAT. ANN. § 7-242(a) (1959).

Psychiatric Exam: Authorized when competency to stand trial or criminal responsibility is raised as an issue. WYO. STAT. ANN. § 7-241 (Supp. 1973).

Statement to Jury Concerning Effect of Acquittal: Defendant has no right to an instruction whether requested or not. *Lonquest v. State*, 495 P.2d 575 (Wyo. 1972).

Post-Acquittal Confinement: Civil commitment proceedings must be instituted if defendant is to be retained after acquittal. WYO. STAT. ANN. § 7-242(b) (1959).

Diminished Responsibility: Evidence of an abnormal mental condition, although not sufficient to establish legal insanity as a complete defense, is admissible for the purpose of determining which crime was committed. *State v. Pressler*, 16 Wyo. 214, 92 P. 806 (1907).

Evidence of an abnormal mental condition is admissible for the purpose of showing that defendant charged with first degree murder did not have the capacity to, or in fact did not, deliberate or premeditate the act at the time the homicide was committed, and that for this reason, only second degree murder was committed. *State v. Pressler*, 16 Wyo. 214, 92 P. 806 (1907).

Table of Cases

Index

Index

About the Author

Grant H. Morris is a professor at the University of San Diego School of Law and an adjunct professor at the University of California, San Diego, School of Medicine. He received the A.B. and J.D. degrees from Syracuse University and the LL.M. degree from Harvard Law School. Professor Morris, who teaches law and psychiatry, is the author of numerous articles exploring the interface of these two disciplines. He is coauthor and editor of *The Mentally Ill and the Right to Treatment*, the first book dealing with the emerging legal right of involuntarily confined mental patients to receive adequate treatment.

Professor Morris has participated in several law revision projects, serving as a staff member of an Institute of Public Administration project to revise the New York Mental Hygiene Law, as Legal Counsel to the Michigan Legislative Committee to Revise the Mental Health Statutes, and as consultant to the Criminal Code Commission of the Arizona State Legislature.

During 1973 and 1974, Professor Morris was Chairperson of the Law and Psychiatry Section of the Association of American Law Schools.